MILWAUKEE MOVIE PALACES

Larry Widen and Judi Anderson

Sponsored by the
Milwaukee Area Technical College
Alumni Association

Milwaukee County Historical Society
1986

ISBN 0-938076-07-8
Library of Congress Catalog Card Number: 86-62585

© 1986
Milwaukee County Historical Society
910 North Old World Third Street
Milwaukee, Wisconsin 53203

Printed in the United States of America

Cover: *The Oriental theater, photo by Larry Widen*

Back Cover: *The Comique theater, photo by Joseph Brown,*
courtesy of Jessie Walker

Printed by the Milwaukee Area Technical College Press
Body copy ten-point Primer. Printed on seventy-pound coated offset.

ACKNOWLEDGMENTS

The authors wish to thank the following individuals for their outstanding guidance, encouragement, and assistance: the late Albert L. Kuhli, Dr. Frederick I. Olson, Daniel D. Reszel, and Hugh W. Swofford.

Thanks also go to the following people for their help in preparing this book: Phillip Balistreri; William Benedict; Carol Best; William Boehnlein; Arnold Brumm; Barnard, Cecelia, and Rudolph Freuler; Gilbert Freundl; Mary Anne Gross; Robert Headley; Fred Hermes; Claire-Lisette Hubbard; William Klinger; Carl Lensce; Frances Maertz; Ben Marcus; the MATC Alumni Association; John Myers; Elmer Nimmer; Paul Oetlinger; Aenone Pitts; Gene Posner; Jeff Posner; James Rankin; George Remlinger; Robert Rothschild; Arnold Saxe; Herman Schmitt; Scott Schultz; Estelle Steinbach; Joe Strother; Bruce Trinz; Edward Trinz; Les Vollmert; Leona Whiteley; Susan Wirth; Wisconsin Heritages, Inc.; Fred Wolfgram; Betty Zagel; and Frank Zeidler.

In addition, the authors wish to extend a very special thank you to Milwaukee County Historical Society Executive Director Harry H. Anderson and the Editorial and Publications Committee for their support of this project.

INTRODUCTION

Motion pictures have been projected to audiences in Milwaukee since 1896, and the compilation of this ninety-year history meant consulting hundreds of sources, many of which offered conflicting information. Bits and pieces were scattered in attics, in city directories, on insurance maps, in newspaper stories, in Building Inspector reports, and in the memories of the city's elderly residents. The latter source was as frustrating as it was valuable, for often we spoke with a son or daughter who was recalling memories of a parent long since deceased.

Because of incomplete or missing records, one of the greatest challenges was to determine the name, location, and operating dates of Milwaukee's first permanent motion picture theater. Until recently, all available evidence gave credit to John and Tom Saxe for being Milwaukee's first motion picture operators at a permanent location. However, we now know that the Saxe brothers, along with Henry Trinz and a host of other adventurous entrepreneurs, were only *among* the first. John Freuler's Comique theater on South Kinnickinnic Avenue was in fact Milwaukee's first permanent motion picture theater, opening on December 5, 1905, preceding the Saxe theater by eight months.

This narrative is not meant to be a history of Milwaukee, but certain factors in the city's past play an important part in telling the story. For example, in 1930 the majority of the street addresses were changed to accommodate the expansion of population and the new city limits. For purposes of simplification, only the current address of a theater is used here, regardless of whether or not the building still exists. For example, the Theatorium, torn down in 1923, had an address of 136 Grand Avenue. If that building were still standing today, its address would be 184 West Wisconsin Avenue, so that is how it is referred to here.

By our definition, a movie theater is an operation that presents moving pictures as its principal function and/or for its major income. However, since vaudeville theaters and legitimate stages were early exhibitors of motion pictures, and several became picture theaters to remain in business, they also have a place in the narrative. For this reason other entertainment operations such as dime museums, penny arcades, and amusement parks that were instrumental in bringing motion pictures to the public are also discussed in the text. In contrast, we do not discuss the "drive-in" theater, as it represents a viewing concept far removed from the movie palace; therefore, it has no place in the narrative.

During the initial stages of our research in June, 1983, the remains of the former Milwaukee theater at 2754 North Teutonia Avenue were demolished. From the once popular neighborhood house we were able to preserve a letter from the marquee and take a few photographs of the demolition. In December, 1983, the Egyptian theater, which had been decaying for over a decade on Teutonia Avenue, was also demolished. From there we were able to save several beautiful plaster castings and one complete seat from the auditorium. In addition, we took the last photographs ever of the interior just before it was razed. In September, 1984, the Princess, Milwaukee's oldest operating movie theater, was torn down after 80 years of continuous service. As the preparation of a final manuscript neared completion in May, 1986, yet another of Milwaukee's grandest theaters was being slated for demolition, the former Wisconsin theater on West Wisconsin Avenue. After a long struggle to remain commercially viable, the Carpenter Building, which housed Milwaukee's first true "movie palace," had been purchased by a wrecking company and was awaiting destruction.

The alarming rate at which these old landmarks have been disappearing was a primary reason for getting this text and collection of photographs together.

After going through some tough times in the 1950s and 1960s, the movies and their theaters still flourish today, but attitudes about moviegoing have changed. What was once a total escape to elegance and fantasy has become a two-hour stopover in a barren shopping center shoebox. The quality of some multiplex cinema auditoriums bears a strong resemblance to the early nickelodeon storefront theaters, despite the fact that movies today are more technically advanced than anyone in 1906 could have imagined.

The Avalon theater, the Oriental theater, the former Warner theater (now the Grand 1 & 2), and the newly renovated Riverside theater are the last reminders of the splendor that was once a part of going to the movies. This history is meant to insure that these theaters, and the others no longer standing, are remembered forever.

—*Judi Anderson and Larry Widen*
June, 1986

Milwaukee Movie Palaces

CONTENTS

CHAPTER 1

MILWAUKEE'S EARLY AMUSEMENTS
1842-1904

I N 1842, WITH WISCONSIN'S Potawatomi Indians still inhabiting their Lime Ridge Village near the present 20th Street and Clybourn Street, John Hustis built Milwaukee's first legitimate theater. Four years before Milwaukee was even chartered as a city, a theater troupe from Chicago presented the first local stage performance, "The Merchant of Venice," at the John Hustis theater on the corner of Third Street and Juneau Avenue.

At a time when men worked six to seven days a week and women ran the family home without the benefit of what we now consider to be necessities, leisure time was at a premium. Social life often centered around the church, and an evening's entertainment was a well-deserved reward for many days of hard labor.

In the 1840s, Milwaukee was growing at a rate of almost 2,000 residents a year. The small town of 1,700 residents in 1840 had exploded into a booming metropolis of over 20,000 by 1850. The new population, many of whom were immigrants, had a taste for quality entertainment that only a large city could offer. The John Hustis theater was soon facing competition for audiences as other entrepreneurs began to open theaters of their own.

By 1865, elegance was added to theatergoing when the Academy of Music was opened at East Michigan Street and North Broadway to more fully accommodate high quality traveling theatrical companies. In 1872, patrons flocked to performances at the opulent Grand Opera House on the present site of the Pabst theater.

However, theater performances were not enough for the hard-working citizens of Milwaukee, and a variety of other entertainment forms sprang up to accommodate all levels of taste. Soon, residents were able to spend their spare time at amusement parks and dime museums, and viewing the famous panorama paintings.

The panoramas were a short-lived but extremely popular entertainment phenomenon that proved to be a tremendous attraction, beginning in the 1880s. They are considered by some to be the forerunners of moving pictures because of the subjects of the paintings, as well as the manner in which they were exhibited.

The first panorama paintings were shown in music halls and theaters by traveling companies that specialized in their presentation. The oil paintings were often hundreds of feet long and took hours to unroll from a large wooden spool. The subjects presented included famous battles, fires, and religious scenes, such as "The Expulsion of Adam and Eve From Paradise." With live musical accompaniment, the paintings were slowly unrolled before an audience as the narrator explained what was happening in each scene.

The panoramas soon became popular enough to warrant a permanent showplace. Milwaukee had two; the first was at

The Panorama Building at N. 6th St.

North Sixth Street and Kilbourn Avenue. Nearby, on Wells Street between Sixth and Seventh Streets, was a large studio where the panoramas were produced and which was later used for exhibition purposes.

A group of German painters settled here in 1885 to paint panoramas that would be sold throughout the United States. These massive canvases often took a dozen artists six to eight months to complete at a total cost of more than $25,000.

For the more famous paintings, such as "General Grant's Assault on Vicksburg" and the battles of Lookout Mountain and Atlanta, extensive research was done, and several artists were dispatched to the actual battle site to reproduce terrain for the final product in an authentic manner. After the sketches were completed, they were projected onto a canvas and the images were drawn in and painted. The final step before opening to the public was to add rocks, trees, fences, and actual soil in the front of the painting to create a realistic, three-dimensional diorama.

The result was a painted canvas fifty feet high and 350 to 400 feet long that was on continuous exhibit for a year or more in the panorama building. On July 4, 1885, the depiction of "Grant's Assault" was unveiled to an enthusiastic public who gladly paid fifty cents to view it. (Ironically the newspapers were running headlines that Grant was dying in New York at the same time the panorama was opening.)

Inside the panorama, the Vicksburg show commenced with lecturer James Larkin giving a splendid account of the famous battle. As he told the story, the appropriate section of the huge canvas was illuminated, thereby drawing the complete attention of the audience to that particular scene. The talk continued in this manner until all areas of the canvas had been exposed. *The Milwaukee Journal* and *Sentinel* ran favorable reviews, and local veterans of the battle agreed that it was an accurate depiction down to the most minute details.

Despite the popularity of the panoramas, the amusement had died out by 1890. And when motion pictures were projected in 1896, any hopes of a panorama revival were dashed. Several Milwaukee artists went to California in 1899 to produce a version of "Dewey's Victory at Manila Bay," but its popularity was short lived. The painters later were able to find other work locally, such as creating murals for the Milwaukee Turner Hall walls, stage scenery for the Pabst, Alhambra, and Bijou theaters, and many private commissions.

Opposite: Panorama artist and model on the Mitchell Building roof

Another form of theater amusement did extremely well on the premise that it offered an incredible amount of entertainment for ten cents. The dime museums were destined to exist for only a short time, but while they were around, the theaters and curio halls of the museums were the best value for hours of entertainment.

These houses were named for the ten-cent standard admission price and also to distinguish themselves from the more conservative public museum located at the Milwaukee Exposition Building. The attractions at the dime museums were anything but conservative, and their aim was to display and perhaps flaunt the most outrageous exhibits.

In March, 1884, a young theatrical entrepreneur named

The European Museum, 152 W. Wisconsin Ave.

Jacob Litt was appointed manager of the Schlitz Park theater. The park, located at 7th and Walnut Streets, was a favorite summer place to hear music and opera. In addition to booking a season of concerts for the park theater, Litt set about establishing a quality dime museum adjoining the park's opera house. The museum was billed as a safe place for parents to leave their children as well as an enjoyable experience for adults. Litt boasted that the new museum had an "extensive menagerie and numerous living creatures in addition to an hourly stage show."

Jacob Litt

The Schlitz Park museum proved to be so popular that its proceeds enabled Litt to purchase the failing Grand Avenue Dime Museum at 172 West Wisconsin Avenue, across from the Plankinton House hotel, now the site of the Plankinton Arcade. Under Litt's direction, the museum was completely overhauled and repainted. Private boxes were installed on either side of the stage, and a direct alarm was hooked up to the fire station in case of fire. In addition, policemen were on hand to preserve order and to discourage the "mashers" who were known to annoy museum patrons.

In its first year of operation, Litt's Grand Avenue Dime Museum netted over $17,000, a princely sum in those days. Because Litt had contracts with St. Louis and Chicago museums, he was able to book the best acts for his shows, choosing from a variety of national attractions.

In addition to a permanent display hall, the museum featured a stage show that changed weekly, often with ten acts scheduled on the bill. Typical museum fare was advertised in the *Sentinel* for the week of October 11, 1885. It stated that Litt's Mammoth Dime Museum was offering the "Queerest, Quaintest Atom of Humanity Ever on Display." The "atom" was an attraction called the Turtle Boy, a rather homely little midget who sat on a pedestal and carried on an amusing round of chatter for viewers. Also on that bill were the Bewitching Albino Sisters Whose Flowing White Hair Reaches Below Their Waists, and Belle Moody, the Human Billiard Ball. Curio Hall exhibits included odd mechanical contraptions and devices, items of a historical nature, and various specimens of animal mutations preserved in glass laboratory jars. The featured display was the Murderer's Cabinet, a col-

LITT'S MILWAUKEE MAMMOTH MUSEUM.

OPEN DAILY FROM 1 TO 10 P. M.

ON MONDAY, JANUARY 11,

FAT WOMEN'S CONVENTION

WILL BEGIN ITS SESSION. Promptly at 1:30 o'clock the choice of seats will be allotted, and the CONVOCATION OF COMELY CORPULENTS will immediately commence electioneering for votes, each eagerly endeavoring to outstrip the others for the

3 DIAMOND ENCRUSTED PRIZES 3

——Which will be——

PRESENTED to the PORTLY PILGRIMS!

Who receive the most Ballots.

ALL PREVIOUS FAT WOMEN CONVENTIONS WERE MERE CAUCUSES compared with this ENDEARING, ENCHANTING, ENTERTAINING

Round-up of Richly Robed Rotundity!!

Which consists of

30 FAMOUS FAT FEMALES 30

Comprising all of the NOTED PRIZE WINNERS OF TWO CONTINENTS. FRISKY FASHIONABLES clad in Gorgeous Silken Raiment, and Bedecked with Priceless Gems, will coyly contest for supremacy with their more HUMBLE ASSOCIATES whose apparel was Not Designed by Worth and who wear Rhine Stones.

The Feather-Weight of the Meeting Tips the Beam at 465 pounds, and several others

WEIGH OVER ONE-THIRD OF A TON.

MILWAUKEE'S MONSTER MAIDEN

Will Actively Compete with their OBESE OUTSIDE OPPONENTS.

3 VALUABLE PRIZES 3

Are to be awarded to the Trio who receive the most votes.

VOTE WHENEVER YOU FEEL LIKE IT.

Sommers & Walters Eccentric Comedy Co.

Will Blithely Cater for your Amusement IN THE BIJOU THEATRE,

10c ADMITS YOU 10c

And Entitles You to Vote.

lection of devices supposedly used to commit various homicides.

In the fall of 1889, Jacob Litt announced that he was discontinuing his dime museum at the first of the year since the business was no longer profitable enough for him. The announcement came just after the opening of Litt's newest and more legitimate theatrical venture.

In March, 1889, architect Oscar Cobb was awarded the contract to build Jacob Litt's dream theater, the Bijou opera house. Located on North 2nd Street near Michigan Street, the Bijou was a stunning tour de force for the young man who entered show business via the dime museums.

On Monday evening, August 17, 1889, the twenty-year-old Litt saw his Bijou become a reality. Architect Cobb was present, having come from Chicago to attend the opening festivities of the 175th theater he had designed in the country. The Bijou seated 1,800 people in a temple derived primarily from Moorish origins. The auditorium ceiling was blue with clusters of incandescent lights resembling stars, among which floated depictions of Cupid and other mythological creatures. Motion pictures were first shown on the premises in 1900 when Litt presented "Night Views of the Hudson" and "Pictures of the Williamsburg Bridge" at the end of a seven-unit vaudeville show. In the late 1920's, the Bijou was renamed the Garrick and showed motion pictures until the building was torn down in 1931.

In its review of the Bijou, the *Milwaukee Sentinel* said, "The pitch of the floors are such that those in front will not obscure the view of those in the rear; that is, if the members of the gentle sex are considerate enough not to wear hats of unpardonable dimensions. Long-suffering mankind is looking forward to the day when Dame Fashion requires that no hats be worn."

In 1892, a frustrated young actor/comedian named Otto Meister left his job as clerk for the Goodrich Transportation Company and found work in the dime museums. He began as a barker at the newly opened Wonderland museum on North 3rd Street. The Wonderland was owned by Byron Burton, a former carpenter and hotel proprietor from Joliet, Illinois. Burton bought all of Jacob Litt's museum stock from storage in August, 1892, and together with his sons Frank and Dow operated the new enterprise.

With the Burton trio at the helm and Meister in the street,

Wonderland made it through the 1892-93 season. When it re-opened in the fall of 1893, Meister was working inside as an assistant manager as well as a featured performer. His specialty was standup comedy done with an exaggerated German accent and a large walking stick. Several weeks into the season, owner Burton died. His unexpected death occurred on November 7, the very evening that a future show business legend opened a week-long stand at the museum.

The act consisted of seventeen-year-old Erich (or Erlich) Weiss, and his younger brother Theo, who billed themselves as the "Houdini Brothers and the Mystery Box." Erich Weiss went on to international fame using the name Harry Houdini and always retained an affection for Milwaukee. Meister also stayed in show business his entire life, going on to open the Vaudette, the Magnet, the Butterfly, and the White House theaters.

Otto Meister

The mid-1890s saw Meister and other dime museum men exhibiting a countless variety of acts, each one billed as better than the last. The Star museum, which later became the Star theater, and the Columbia on 3rd Street, featured novelties such as the Skating Horse and the Iron-Skulled Man, who broke bricks on his head. Other popular attractions were freaks such as the Armless Landscape Painter, the Legless Acrobat, and the Dog-Faced Boy. In addition to the oddities and curiosities, there were endless numbers of mind readers, magicians, balladeers, speedy whittlers and clay modelers, dancers, gymnasts, musicians, and elocutionists.

But the winds of change were blowing in the entertainment world, and both the Star and the Columbia lasted less than one year. On Sunday, July 26, 1896, Thomas Edison's new invention, the Vitascope, made its appearance at the Academy of Music theater located at Broadway and Michigan Street. The event marked the first time that a motion picture had ever been projected before an audience in the city.

Of the premiere, a *Milwaukee Sentinel* reviewer stated that "the Academy was literally crowded to the doors at both performances yesterday, hundreds being turned away from the evening performance before 8:00 p.m. Undoubtedly, the great attendance was caused by the announcement that Edison's wonderful invention, the Vitascope, would be seen in this city for the first time."

The pictures presented included a New York City elevated

train platform with arriving and departing trains, the celebrated "kiss" between Mae Irwin and John Rice, and a boxing match with Gentleman Jim Corbett and a hapless opponent. The *Sentinel* reporter (and the audience) appeared to be most impressed by a scene in which the surf rolled along a stone pier, the waves seeming to break in the viewer's lap. He wrote: "The effects were wonderful, and each scene was received with loud applause, and encores were demanded in every instance." A reviewer from *The Milwaukee Journal* had similar praise and added that "in simple explanation of this astounding apparatus, it may be said that it is the same as the kinetoscope excepting that the images are thrown upon a screen in the manner of a magic lantern, and they are life-sized. Certainly it is a wonderful sight and should not be missed by anyone during its short appearance here."

Until the perfection of the Vitascope, only one person at a time could view the tiny, flickering kinetoscope images in darkened penny arcades. Now, large motion picture images with impact could be presented to an audience for better profits to owners. The rapidity with which people responded to the

Milwaukee Sentinel advertisement, June 26, 1896

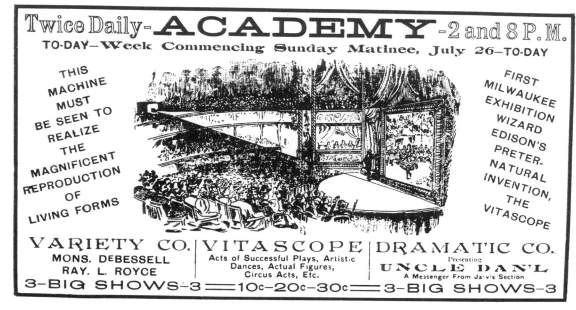

Legitimate theaters were featuring motion pictures by 1900

new form of motion pictures spelled the beginning of the end for entertainments such as the dime museum, much in the same way that talking pictures reduced the public interest in vaudeville shows after 1927.

Several entertainment men in Milwaukee were quick to recognize the potential profit from exhibiting moving pictures. The Academy of Music had several repeat performances of the Vitascope before the end of 1896, and by March, 1897, the management had instituted weekly showings of films under the billing "Magnascope." In November, 1897, Otto Meister presented a variety of films at his Phanta-Phone and Nickelodeon theaters, located at 212 West Wisconsin Avenue. The Phanta-Phone was a short-lived experiment by Meister attempting to combine the acts of a dime museum with penny-operated phonograph and kinetoscope machines, as well as the projection of a variety of moving picture scenes. The Phanta-Phone was in business for less than two months when

Meister decided to revamp it into a more conventional theater. The result was the Nickelodeon theater, which opened just after Christmas. Ironically, the Phanta-Phone and the Nickelodeon were located on the very site that would house Meister's Butterfly theater in 1911.

Another theatrical manager to get involved with motion pictures was Oscar Miller, who booked the Biograph Company's films at the Alhambra in the summer of 1898. Entitled "Views of the Spanish American War," the pictures were changed every three or four weeks and were an early version of the newsreels that were a staple on theater programs in the years before television.

By 1899, moving pictures were being shown throughout the city in halls, theaters, museums, churches, and outdoor amusement parks. Milwaukee had several popular parks near the turn of the century, and all of them were early exhibitors of moving pictures. Shoot-the-Chutes Park, located on the river at North and Cambridge Avenues, was the first such park to feature Biograph pictures in 1898 in its vaudeville house located on the grounds. Larger parks, such as Oscar Miller's Coney Island in Shorewood, presented motion pictures as one of many attractions.

Despite Miller's allegiance to the Alhambra, he invested heavily in other entertainment ventures, such as the development of a massive amusement park at Mineral Springs on the Milwaukee River. Today the area once occupied by Miller's park is the site of Hubbard Park in Shorewood, but in the early 1900s, it was a popular place that featured a giant roller coaster, water slides, a vaudeville theater, circus acts, penny arcades, tintype parlors, beer gardens, restaurants, a ferris wheel, a museum, and an "electric theater," just to show moving pictures. The park changed hands in 1904 and became known as Wonderland, and later, Ravenna Park.

Many traveling circuses, the State Fair, and the summer parks such as White City near Washington Park also featured an electric theater in their newspaper advertisements. When the picture theater boom occurred in 1906, many of the owners incorporated the word "electric" into the name of the theater.

The exhibition of boxing films proved to be a popular attraction, and they were first presented by veteran theater man John Slensby in September, 1899, at his Trocadero theater at 730 North 3rd Street. "Boxing Pictures Projected by the

Cinematographe" proved so popular that larger theaters such as the Alhambra, Crystal, and Davidson began to show them on occasion, featuring entire bouts from regional and national competitions.

In 1904, the first in a series of revolutions in the motion picture exhibition industry came about at the World's Fair in St. Louis. Kansas City fire chief George Hale unveiled his motion picture invention which would soon become known as Hale's Tours. The "tour" was actually an illusion that used moving pictures to create the sensation of traveling across the world.

The setup consisted of a platform on which were mounted

Pabst Park at N. Third and W. Burleigh Sts.

fifty seats. The platform was constructed to resemble the interior of a railroad car, with a device underneath that gently rocked the platform to create the feeling of motion. To this were added the pictures, so that when the riders looked at the various scenes of the world, they felt as if they were viewing them from a real train. To add to the realism, the ticket taker acted as a conductor, calling out stops, ringing bells, and blowing whistles.

This tour car created excitement all over the country, and many amusement parks bought the franchise to add to their existing operation. In Milwaukee, Hale's Tours became a popular drawing card as well as a big moneymaker for the Wonderland amusement park.

CHAPTER 2

THE NICKELODEON YEARS
1905-1911

JOHN R. FREULER WAS a Milwaukee real estate man with offices in the prestigious Matthews Building on West Wisconsin Avenue. To someone of his social standing, the motion pictures were considered to be a cheap and vulgar form of entertainment to be enjoyed by low-income residents who could not afford to attend legitimate stage performances.

In 1905, the opportunity presented itself for Freuler to invest in what would be Milwaukee's first permanent motion picture theater, his investment of $400 being the only way he could insure collection of an outstanding debt. When the unimposing Comique theater opened at 2246 South Kinnickinnic Avenue on December 5, 1905, Freuler was involved, grudgingly, for fifty percent of the ownership.

In the beginning, Freuler said nothing to his family about his association with a moving picture theater, and he actually turned his head as he passed the theater, lest someone suspect his interest. But in the weeks that followed, Freuler began to find excuse after excuse to pass by the Comique, and soon he stopped in daily to check on the operations. Within six months after being forced to invest in this venture, Freuler

Opposite: The Comique, 1905

had gone from being a silent partner to taking an active hand in shaping the theater's future. He then bought his partner out and became sole owner and operator of the Comique.

After running the theater for a short time, Freuler realized that he could make a great deal of money by supplying films to other theater owners as well as showing them himself. He reasoned correctly that if a film distributorship were located in town, exhibitors would be apt to rent more films and change their programs more often.

On July 1, 1906, the Western Film Exchange was created in Freuler's real estate office. Soon the company was renting films to beer gardens, summer parks, and legitimate houses such as the Bijou, Alhambra, Crystal, and Star, as well as to the storefront picture theaters that were beginning to appear on the city's busiest streets.

Freuler later went on to organize two motion picture studios, the North American Film Company in 1910 and the Mutual Film Corporation in 1912. Freuler was the president of Mutual until 1918 and operated 68 subsidiary companies out of his Chicago office which supplied 7,000 theaters across the United States with films each week.

But in Milwaukee, he began by encouraging the owners of the new storefront picture theaters to change their film programs three, four, and even five times each week. These earliest picture theaters were dubbed "nickelodeons" in the east, and the name caught on. By combining the price of admission with "odeon," the Greek word for theater, a nickname was born that spread like wildfire.

John Freuler

The first nickelodeons were extremely consistent in design — former storefronts that were unadorned except for camp chairs or wooden benches arranged in rows. The more rustic operations even had dirt floors. The "screen" was often no more than a white wall or a sheet nailed at the corners. These picture parlors, as they were referred to on building permits, accommodated from 50 to 200 people at a time. They had little or no light, poor ventilation, and two tiny aisles in case of fire. Some of the facilities in the outlying areas were so primitive that during intermission the back yard or alley served as the rest room for both sexes.

Though the interiors were barren, the exteriors were often resplendent. This was a time when patrons had to be sufficiently enticed to enter the newfangled moving picture houses, and the facades and outside decor helped to do just that. Hundreds of light bulbs and an abundance of photos and posters were employed in an effort to lure the customer to the point of parting with five cents. Early theater owners who promoted their wares too enthusiastically found themselves paying fines of one to five dollars for violation of the city's billboard ordinances. Under the Milwaukee code, theaters could not display any advertising matter in public view that contained artwork or photography of a lurid or violent nature. Women especially were not to be seen on posters in any sort of compromising situation, and many budding movie entrepreneurs learned this the hard way.

A typical nickelodeon facade

At the turn of the century, Tom and John Saxe had invested in a dime museum, and later a penny arcade. Both attempts failed, and after each one, the brothers went back to their respective trades of painting signs and running a saloon. In the fall of 1906, the Saxes made another effort to enter the entertainment business by purchasing the franchise for operating a Hale's Tours ride in Milwaukee. They leased a storefront at 184 West Wisconsin Avenue and installed the amusement under the name Scenes of the World.

The operation was a great success with the public, who flocked in great numbers to marvel at the frequently changed views from around the world. The shows ran fifteen minutes each and admission was five cents. The turnover was rapid, and the Saxes were able to run several dozen showings each day. The unqualified success that accompanied this latest foray into entertainment was the turning point in the Saxe

The Saxe Brothers' first theater

brothers' lives and set into motion the beginning of their future as Milwaukee's movie magnates.

Next to Wisconsin Avenue, the busiest shopping district in the city was on Mitchell Street, and several moving picture houses began to appear in the blocks between 6th and 12th Streets. People with no previous experience were leasing storefronts and converting them into theaters. A relatively small investment could purchase the simple projection equipment and seating arrangements that were necessary to embark on a career in moving pictures. These were naive times with no proven standards to guide the budding entrepreneurs. Many entered the business with courage, high hopes, and $300. There were a few success stories, but many more failures.

Among the early trailblazers on Mitchell Street was Edward Wagner, a laborer who was dissatisfied with his job working for someone else. He saw the moving pictures as a chance to finally go into a business for himself. Wagner and his wife Martha opened the Emporium in July, 1906, at 626 West Mitchell Street. Shortly after opening, Wagner renamed his theater the Imperial 5¢ Theater, just to make sure that everyone knew about the fine entertainment at a reasonable rate. Even so, the nickel of 1906 bought many of the same things that four dollars does today.

It is easy to see why only the most innovative and dedicated operators were able to keep their theaters open amid all the competition. Wagner continued to stay in the theater business until his death in 1930 while running the Garden theater in South Milwaukee. After using the Mitchell Street theater as a beginning, Wagner and his family became involved in running the Happy Hour theater on Muskego Avenue, the Park theater on Mitchell Street, and the Wagner theater on Forest Home Avenue.

Not all the Mitchell Street pioneers were as lucky as the Wagners. The Dietrich brothers, a trio of piano salesmen, closed their music store and opened the Unique Electric theater at 10th and Mitchell Streets in February, 1907. The Unique was unique in that it had only seventy-three seats and closed within three months.

Moving picture theaters began to include the term "electric" after their name so people would instantly know that the the-

The Lincoln theater, 1104 W. Lincoln Ave.

ater specialized in pictures rather than live performances. Consequently, Milwaukee for a time had an abundance of theaters such as the Iola Electric, the Union Electric, the Unique Electric, and the Electric Joy.

The area's most prominent exhibitor, Henry Trinz, began on Mitchell Street with the Trinz Electric theater. Trinz and his brothers had operated a saloon in Chicago for Milwaukee's Schlitz Brewery until 1905. He moved to Milwaukee early in 1906 and settled near 12th and Mitchell Streets. Henry invested $700 and opened his electric theater at 1202 West Mitchell Street in April, 1906. His success there allowed him to open theaters on Kinnickinnic, Lincoln, and Fond du Lac Avenues that were operated by brothers Aaron, Samuel, and Joseph. In the summer of 1906, Schlitz invested heavily in the Trinz brothers' Empire theater, a large picture and vaudeville house at 1125 West Mitchell Street. Once the Empire was in operation, the brothers bought the former West Side Turn Hall at 1023 West Walnut Street and converted it for motion pictures as the Columbia.

Henry Trinz

The Trinz operation grew larger, and by 1914 they were operating the Avenue theater at Lincoln and Howell Avenues, the Savoy at 27th and Center Streets, and the Star at 15th Street and Fond du Lac Avenue in addition to the Columbia and the Empire. By 1920, the Trinz brothers divested themselves of their Milwaukee holdings and took their operations to Chicago where they bought into the Balaban and Katz chain, keeping Trinz heirs prominent in Chicago theatrical management until the mid-1970s.

At the same time that the Trinz brothers, Edward Wagner, and a host of others were competing at a furious pace, the Saxe brothers were assessing the profits from their Scenes of the World theater and contemplating their next move. They both agreed that it was time to expand their moving picture operation and felt they could do without the added expense of the Hale's Tours franchise. The brothers disengaged themselves from the contract with Hale and set about remodeling the little theater at 184 West Wisconsin Avenue into a larger operation.

The result was a 242-seat house called the Theatorium. It was the largest moving picture theater to date in Milwaukee, as well as the cleanest and safest. It had reasonably comfortable seats that were securely bolted to the floor, and two large aisles, each with an exit. The outside was embellished with two mythological figures guarding the entrance and a ticket booth that was shaped like a Moorish minaret. The Theatorium opened each day at noon and presented ten shows, each lasting just under an hour. The program included illustrated songs, a lecture, and several short films, all for five cents.

The theater was a success from the start, and while Tom Saxe saw to the operations of the theater, John looked around for another property that they could develop in a similar manner. He found an opportunity right across the street at John Callahan's billiard hall. Callahan was a pool hall operator who had been on Wisconsin Avenue for years and had recently tried to expand his business to include a theater and penny arcade at 203 West Wisconsin Avenue. Things were not going well, and Callahan sold his Theater Delight to the Saxe brothers in 1907. They completely renovated the hall and named it the Orpheum, with plans to showcase moving pictures interspersed with vaudeville acts.

The Orpheum had 340 seats, nearly 100 more than the Theatorium across the street. By playing different sets of pictures at each theater, the Saxes assured themselves of filling both houses with patrons hungry for the new medium of entertainment. As eager as they were to expand again, the brothers were also extremely shrewd businessmen who avoided the mistake of trying to get too far too fast. Rather than open three or four theaters and see them all faltering, Tom and John opted instead to carefully cultivate each new enterprise until it could stand on its own before moving on to the next. In this manner, they slowly but surely built a solid empire of theaters that would make them *the* force to be reckoned with in Milwaukee's theatrical world.

In late 1907, the Saxes set their sights on a small Edison parlor at 1220 West Walnut Street. Managed by the elderly Schultz brothers, another team of would-be movie entrepreneurs, the Edison parlor was a fancy penny arcade where patrons activated coin-operated phonographs and vitascopes. The operation was very similar to the one that the Saxes had tried to run in 1902 with little luck. They bought the outdated amusement parlor from the Schultzes and commissioned architect John Menge, Jr., to convert the entire building into an attractive picture theater which they named the Globe.

Thomas Saxe

In 1907, Walnut Street was a bustling district of shops, restaurants, and recreational outlets, making it an attractive place to open a picture theater. With the success of the Globe assured, the brothers bought a theater at 311 West Wisconsin Avenue, located in the Matthews Building, where Woolworth's is today. They remodeled the facility and opened it to the public in mid-1908 as the Lyric.

*Original facade of
the Princess*

Although 1908 was the year they acquired their fourth theater, it was more importantly the year that the Saxe brothers incorporated their business into a firm known as Saxe Amusement Enterprises (hereafter Saxe AE). Upon forming their corporation, the brothers officially became the leading exhibitors of moving pictures in the city.

The process of acquiring and renovating existing nickelodeons came to a climax for Saxe AE in December, 1909, when it opened the Princess theater at 738 North 3rd Street. The Princess was not a newly constructed theater, but rather an extensive renovation of the already existing Grand theater. The Grand opened in May, 1904, as a family vaudeville house owned by the Pabst Brewery. In 1908 the theater dropped its live performance policy and presented moving pictures under the direction of the O. T. Crawford Company, a firm that leased similar theaters for shows in Denver, St. Louis, Cleveland, and other major cities. In October, 1909, the Crawford lease was not renewed, and Saxe AE gained control of the theater. It immediately removed all vestiges of the former Grand theater, leaving only the walls. The stage was torn out and the length of the theater was extended twenty-five feet in the rear to accommodate a new, larger stage and proscenium.

Under the administration of architect Henry Lotter, the Saxe brothers spent over $50,000 to remodel a theater that had cost only $10,000 to build six years earlier. Renovations in the theater included the addition of four private boxes, a balcony, and a luxurious decor that was previously unheard of in a moving picture theater. When it opened on December 17, 1909, the Princess was unquestionably the most elegant movie house in town and was instrumental in changing the attitudes of many in favor of picture theaters.

The Princess seated 900 people, and on opening night it was packed with a specially selected audience of city officials, rival theater managers, and members of Milwaukee society. Mayor David S. Rose delivered the dedicatory address at the beginning of the evening's program, and Thomas Saxe told the *Sentinel* that "this invitation affair was given in an effort

Princess ad, 1909

PRINCESS 10

THIS WEEK

NEW PICTURE DRAMAS
NEW SONGS and BALLADS
NEW TRAVEL TALKS
NEW SCENIC VIEWS
NEW ORGAN MUSIC
NEW COMEDY PICTURES
and the Famous
PRINCESS ORCHESTRA.

Extra Performances New Year's Day

CENTS

*The nickelodeon-era
Modjeska*

to secure the patronage of a better class of people." With the
moving picture theaters under fire from city fathers, clergy,
and concerned citizens, Saxe AE wanted to assure everyone
that the Princess would be a safe, wholesome environment in
which to view pictures.

As the previewing audience arrived, female ushers in
cadet-grey uniforms showed them to richly upholstered seats.
A $5,000 pipe organ, the city's first theater organ, entertained
while another Milwaukee first, an electric ventilation system,
continuously freshened the air. The program featured music
by the five-piece house orchestra, a solo on the pipe organ, a
group sing-along to illustrated slides, and a variety of short
films. An early trade paper, *The Nickelodeon*, said that "no
better example could be presented for emulation by other
exhibitors than the Milwaukee Princess."

Even with a ten-cent admission, twice that of all the other
picture theaters, the new Princess was a resounding success.
It seemed that people were willing to pay the extra money just
to sit in the splendor of the theater, a fact that Tom Saxe
noted and filed away for use at a later date.

The next year Saxe AE opened a sister theater to the Princess at 1124 West Mitchell Street. Nearly identical in outward appearance, the new theater was called the Modjeska to honor the great Polish actress and the Polish population that lived in the surrounding neighborhood.

While between 1907 and 1910 the moving picture theaters gained in popularity (by 1910 Milwaukee had sixty-four movie theaters operating), it was also the time of increasing criticism of them. Reformers, social workers, and church groups all feared the new moving pictures would lead to the country's moral decay. There was a nationwide movement to censor the theaters, and in 1907 a "Closed Sunday" law went on the books in major cities across the United States. Stemming from a panic over the new moving picture houses, the law prohibited any form of entertainment on Sundays. This included vaudeville, operatic concerts, motion picture showings at the YMCA, or even a scholarly lecture. When a raid to enforce the law occurred in Milwaukee, all present were arrested, including the manager, employees, patrons, and even the electrician.

Another example of this "blue law" movement in Milwaukee was a neighborhood petition circulated in 1910 in an

Early storefront theaters were soon outmoded

*The Cozy, 1036 E.
Brady St.*

attempt to prohibit the licensing of a new nickel theater on the corner of South 8th and Mitchell Streets. The petition, signed by twenty-one area residents, asked that building inspector Edward Koch not grant the theater a license on the grounds that it would be a nuisance on the primarily residential street. The petition stated, "It is a well-known fact that the nickel theater attracts a noisy and boisterous crowd, many of whom congregate on the outside of the theater before, during, and after a performance, and so demean themselves as to render residences in the same block unfit and unbearable as homes." Despite the petition, the Central theater was granted its license and remained in business until 1952 under such names as the Midget and the Popularity before closing as the Delta theater.

Even with the unending criticism, it was not until 1911 that Milwaukee actually began to pass ordinances and zoning regulations for theaters. The first action was to regulate the operation of film projectors as well as the construction, alteration, or remodeling of any building intended for use as a moving picture theater. In 1912 a new division was organized in the City Inspection Office for the sole purpose of theater inspection. Those theaters that did not conform to the new city codes were fined or closed altogether. Ordinances and regulations were also passed concerning the handling and storage of the dangerously flammable nitrate film.

The continued attendance at the Princess and Modjeska theaters proved that the upgrading of moving picture theaters appealed to the public. Other exhibitors soon realized that the storefront nickelodeons were no longer acceptable and, to survive, they must follow the trend toward bigger and better houses or fall by the wayside. The business of exhibiting moving pictures had already come a long way since 1906. With the explosion in popularity of the films and theaters, there was no room for those naive investors possessing only determination and a white sheet for the wall.

Show business veteran Otto Meister had been exhibiting pictures at his Vaudette theater on 3rd Street since 1908 and was netting about $19,000 a year for his efforts. He had been watching the crowds at the Princess across the street for some time, all the while planning a competitive defense. Meister formed the Central Amusement Company with John Freuler in the spring of 1911, and the two concocted a theater for moving pictures that existed only in someone's wildest dreams. They took out a 99-year lease on the land at 212 West Wisconsin Avenue and proceeded to tear down the building then on the premises, the same one that had housed Meister's Nickelodeon and Phanta-Phone theaters in 1898. Construction of the Meister/Freuler theater began in June, 1911, and was completed by the end of August.

On September 2, the pair opened the doors of their outrageously elegant Butterfly theater to great public acclaim.

With 1,500 seats, 3,000 light bulbs, red velvet, and dazzling gold leaf, the interior of the Butterfly was an amazing amalgamation that left nothing to the imagination. Canaries in gilded cages chirped in the lobby as patrons passed to the auditorium. But the real attraction was the theater's namesake, a huge terra cotta butterfly with a human body, that rested on the exterior facade. The spectacular piece measured twenty-seven feet from wingtip to wingtip and was illuminated by 1,000 light bulbs. An additional 2,000 bulbs graced the remainder of the facade.

The Butterfly had a ten-piece house orchestra, a $10,000 pipe organ, and six classically trained opera singers. The ventilation system was promoted as the most modern available and was capable of completely changing the air in the auditorium every three minutes. In addition, Meister and Freuler boasted that their theater was "absolutely fireproof."

The Vaudette grossed $19,000 in its first year

The dazzling elegance of the Butterfly delivered the deathblow to storefront theaters in 1911

The opening night program featured "pictures never before shown in the United States" as well as "side-splitting comedies" and "realistic photo-dramas." If the nickelodeon era suffered a crippling blow with the opening of the Princess, then it surely died on September 2, 1911, at the premiere of the Butterfly. The theaters, like the films they showed, were growing up, and the term "nickelodeon" was fast becoming passé. With nickel admissions and storefront theaters a thing of the past, the new breed of elegant moving picture theaters was being referred to as "photoplay houses"; this reflected both the quality of the theater and the new idea of longer films, or photoplays, that told complete stories.

Otto Meister, presiding over the opening of the Butterfly like a proud father, reached back into his dime museum days and resurrected his 1895 slogan from the Wonderland. The opening advertisement for Meister's Butterfly read, "A dollar show for a dime."

CHAPTER 3

THE PHOTOPLAY HOUSES

THE ADVENT OF THE Princess and Butterfly theaters proved to be representative of a new trend in moving picture houses. The products of the protest and reform movements, they were conceived with a more affluent and upper class clientele in mind. Their luxurious decor, balconies, and box seats were reminiscent of the stylings that had previously been reserved for the legitimate stages. Along with the elegance of the photoplay houses came a new respectability for the motion picture.

The city ordinance published in June, 1911, outlined new rules and specifications for proper lighting, ventilation, exits, and fireproofing of movie theaters. Those who did not comply with the ordinance could be fined up to one hundred dollars or sentenced to up to sixty days' imprisonment. The Butterfly, which opened that September, was the first of many respectable photoplay houses to come out of the reform era and this new ordinance.

To further promote the acceptance of movie houses, the city's motion picture exhibitors waged an all-out promotional campaign in the summer of 1911. By forming what they

Opposite: The fabulous Butterfly

*Milwaukee Journal
ads, June 13, 1911*

called the Exhibitors' League of Milwaukee, they took the first step toward policing their own industry and assuring the public that their theaters were not only safe, but preferred places to go for an hour of entertainment. John Freuler was the first president of the Exhibitors' League and served until 1916, when he was replaced by Henry Trinz. A *Milwaukee Journal* article on June 13, 1911, explained that one of the chief criticisms of moving picture shows of the past had been that their darkness "gave opportunity for flirtations leading to undesirable acquaintances on the part of young girls and boys."

The problem of a totally darkened theater was alleviated in part by the advent of "daylight pictures." This was simply a brighter picture, due to improved print quality and technological advancements in the field, such as specially designed projection screens and projector bulbs with increased wattage. Milestones in the industry such as these served to increase the popularity of pictures and picture theaters.

Under Freuler's leadership, the Exhibitors' League decided

to enhance the image of their movie theaters by going above and beyond the guidelines set up by the new city ordinance. Tom Saxe, the League's treasurer, stated that "if a girl is insulted in some little place, the police are called in and it hurts every moving picture show in the city. There is not a motion picture man in this city who can afford to allow such a thing to happen." To combat this problem, the league members began to employ responsible elderly men as doorkeepers and ushers to assure adequate protection for young ladies. The league, which solicited membership from every exhibitor in Milwaukee, was largely responsible for upgrading the public image of the city's motion picture theaters.

By the end of 1911, people were beginning to think of the movies as educational tools. *The Milwaukee Journal* helped to further this thinking when it said, "The people are sick of the same old stuff. They want to see new scenes of strange countries, examples of trick photography, high-grade comedy, and scenes from famous plays and books."

The Downer, 1915

With the increasing acceptance of picture theaters by the higher-class citizens of Milwaukee, Saxe AE was encouraged enough to bid $40,000 for the lease of the Alhambra theater, which had been converted from a legitimate stage into an all-movie theater in the summer of 1911.

The Alhambra, at 334 West Wisconsin Avenue, was designed for the Schlitz Brewery by Charles Kirchhoff and opened just before Christmas, 1896. The theater was breathtakingly beautiful, and was constructed at a cost of over $500,000. Opening night at this French-inspired palace saw overflow crowds gasping at the 4,000 electric lights, private boxes, and plush red velvet draperies. Police were called to help turn away the hundreds who could not get in as owners

The Alhambra auditorium

42

Henry, Alfred, and August Uihlein sat in their private box at stage left and watched eleven acts of the highest-class vaudeville.

The Alhambra profited handsomely for the next nine years under the direction of theatrical management wizard Oscar Miller. Although Miller was involved financially in various amusement enterprises, such as the Palace dime museum on 3rd Street and the Coney Island summer park in Shorewood, his first allegiance was to the Alhambra and he personally selected all of the acts that played there. Upon Miller's sudden and untimely death in 1905, the Alhambra, without competent management, began to suffer from a loss of patronage. By 1911 Herman Fehr, the acting manager and one of the owners, feared that Schlitz would have to sell the theater. By chance, Fehr made the acquaintance of Samuel Rothapfel while riding a train to Milwaukee. Rothapfel, better known as "Roxy," was fast becoming a legend in theatrical circles for his ability to breathe new life into dying theaters. Fehr hired Roxy on the spot to come to Milwaukee and save the Alhambra. Roxy arrived in town in June, 1911, and immediately went to work. He told Fehr that there was only one way to put the Alhambra back in the black, and that was to show motion pictures. Hesitantly, Fehr agreed, and under Roxy's supervision the 3,000-seat theater became, for a time, the largest moving picture house in the entire world.

Herman Fehr

Roxy installed a nursery for the convenience of matinee-going mothers. He hired a staff of ushers, installed a projection booth, covered the orchestra pit, and replaced all carpets and draperies with new ones. Roxy then sent out to 1,000 prominent Milwaukeeans a letter that read:

> *Dear Sir, Enclosed please find two tickets for the new Alhambra theater, which will admit yourself and a friend to see the beautiful new theater and the wonderful Italian production, "The Fall of Troy," which cost the producers more than $30,000. Please do not feel that you are obligated to the theater in any way. We merely wish to show you what remarkable advances have been made in motion photography and what a valuable adjunct the moving picture has become as an educator. Respectfully yours, S. L. Rothapfel.*

The Alhambra began its new programming in the summer of 1911, realizing substantial profits each week. This income justified the substantial bid by the Saxe brothers for man-

The Saxe Brothers' Milwaukee Theaters.

THEATORIUM · CRYSTAL · PRINCESS · ALHAMBRA · ORPHEUM · MODJESKA · GLOBE

*The Saxe AE
holdings, 1912*

agement of the new movie house. With the Alhambra securely under their wing, Saxe AE now controlled eight theaters: the Juneau, the Globe, the Princess, the Orpheum, the Theatorium, the Modjeska, the Crystal, and the Alhambra.

As 1912 began, the city's exhibitors temporarily stopped building and expanding, instead working to fortify their holdings and solidify their current positions. The Trinz family still controlled the Columbia, Empire, Avenue, and Savoy, as well as a newer addition, the Rainbow theater at 27th Street and Lisbon Avenue. Edward Wagner was working to spruce up his recent acquisitions in Hartford, Racine, and Waukesha in addition to his Milwaukee theaters. John Freuler and Otto

Meister, through the Central Amusement Company, controlled the Butterfly and the Vaudette, as well as the Atlas theater at 3rd Street and North Avenue, and the Climax theater at 20th Street and Fond du Lac Avenue. Many of the former nickelodeon operators who had not gone with the current trends were either working for someone else or out of the business completely.

The construction of a competitive theater was now so expensive that many operators were seeking the financial assistance of large local companies such as the breweries. The Schlitz interests knew the advantages of investing in a theater; they had financed the Empire at 12th and Mitchell Streets and the New Star on North 3rd Street in 1906. The Miller Brewery was not as deeply involved in theaters at this point; it had only invested in the Juneau at 6th and Mitchell Streets in

Interior of the Juneau

1909. But by 1914, Miller was actively looking to invest in moving pictures, and it began by constructing a $200,000 theater/office complex at 510 West Wisconsin Avenue. The resulting theater was the Strand, billed as the "largest exclusive photoplay house west of New York."

The theater advertised 2,000 seats "for perfect comfort" and the latest projection equipment that produced "pictures without a flicker" and assured "perfect ease on the eyes and nervous system." In addition to the latest in moving picture equipment, the Strand also featured a ventilation system that guaranteed that the "last audience of the night will be assured as springlike an atmosphere as the first audience in the morning." To alleviate fears of a fire panic, a sufficient number of exits were included in the plans so that the entire house could be cleared in one minute without disorder. Finally, to attract patrons who found moving pictures hard on the eyes, the Strand employed the latest designs for construction and placement of the screen to assure ideal viewing conditions for all.

Miller turned the management of the Strand over to Saxe AE and began to plan its next investment. The brewery owned a large parcel of land on the west side of 3rd Street just north of Wisconsin Avenue. Purchased by Frederick Miller in 1910, the land was undeveloped by the brewery until 1916, when the firm decided to build a theater and hotel on the site. Aptly named, the Miller theater opened in 1917 as a combination vaudeville and moving picture theater. Mayor Daniel W. Hoan gave a dedicatory speech at the opening and announced also that Saxe AE would be managing the Miller, "Milwaukee's newest recreation palace." Several months after opening, the Miller's policy began concentrating on motion pictures and vaudeville was dropped.

While Miller was working on its theaters, the Joseph Schlitz Brewing Company began development of a new vaudeville and picture theater at 6th Street and Wisconsin Avenue. Architects Kirchhoff and Rose drew up plans in 1915 for a $350,000 theater/office building that became known as the Palace. Although Schlitz intended the 2,400-seat theater to be a live stage, it only remained so for a dozen years before converting to motion pictures, a policy that would continue until its demise in 1974. (Occasional live performances were scheduled during its motion picture years, however.)

Faced with the flurry of theaters that were opening under

their noses, Otto Meister and John Freuler decided to erect another house on 3rd Street, on the lot directly to the north of their Vaudette theater. Meister obtained the necessary permits to demolish the old Wonderland Scenic theater at 739 North 3rd Street in 1916 and set about planning his newest venture. He hired architect Henry Lotter to design a theater that would be different from everything else that was being built at the time. Meister's experience in the dime museums

The Magnet, 735 N. Third St.

Opposite: The Toy Building housed the Toy theater and a dozen of the city's film exchanges

had taught him the value of a gimmick when it came to selling tickets. Lotter came up with a unique plan that called for the new theater's auditorium to be reversed. Thus, when the customer walked in, instead of facing the screen, he would have his back to it. Originally planning to call his theater the Capitol, Meister changed the name at the last minute to the White House, and advertised it as "The House That's Different."

The planning and execution of the White House took longer than either Meister or Freuler counted on, and to raise emergency cash, they sold the Butterfly theater. The pair still held a ninety-nine-year lease on the Butterfly's land however, and continued this ownership until Warner Brothers paid them handsomely for it in 1930. With funds from the sale of the Butterfly, the White House was completed and opened for business on December 16, 1916. Over the years, the theater gained a reputation as Milwaukee's "flip-flop theater," and Meister was on the job there every day until his death in July, 1944.

Throughout the teens, the movies snowballed in popularity. Films, and their audiences, were becoming more sophisticated, and story subjects ranged from comedy to Cleopatra. Movie stars became household names, and personalities like Mary Pickford, Charlie Chaplin, Gloria Swanson, and Lillian Gish enjoyed new-found fame and wealth from their films. Chaplin and Swanson were two stars discovered by John Freuler and signed to make pictures for Mutual Films. In 1916, Freuler outbid Paramount, Universal, and other studios for the services of Charlie Chaplin. Freuler paid $670,000 to Chaplin in a precedent-setting deal that would eventually become standard within the industry.

Another popular type of comedy was the Keystone Company's films featuring a riotous form of slapstick humor that became a widely imitated movie staple for some time. Also popular was the weekly serial, and the new "cliffhanger" arrived each week at the theaters to keep audiences on the edge of their seats. The American landscape proved to be a ready-made set of unrivaled grandeur for western films, and the popular horror film genre can also trace its roots back to this age of moviemaking.

In Milwaukee, Otto Meister was creating a trend of his own, with his clever advertising and displays for the Mack Sennett comedies that played at the Vaudette and White House thea-

Charlie Chaplin and John Freuler, 1916

ters. The word of Meister's extraordinary success soon reached Hollywood, and he became a hero to Sennett and his repertory company. When Meister visited the movie capital in 1917, Sennett showed his gratitude by featuring Meister in a comedy called "Droppington's Family Tree."

Major film studios began to produce films that cost

The Kosciuszko,
1915

$100,000 and reaped over ten times that amount in profits. John Freuler's Mutual Films was one of the original investors in "Birth of a Nation," which opened in 1915 to public acclaim. During its premier run, the film grossed over fifteen

The Merrill

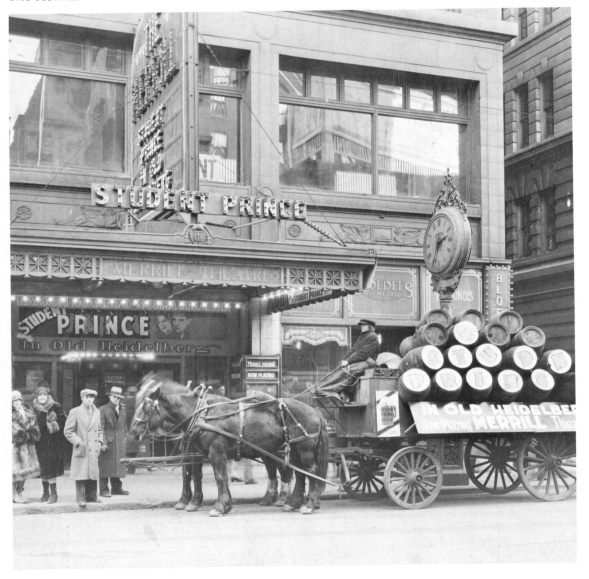

million dollars, due largely to inflated admission prices for the special epic. "Birth of a Nation" also made even the harshest critics of moving pictures sit up and take notice, for the undreamed-of realism and D. W. Griffith's masterful direction were proof that the motion picture was a serious art form.

In 1921, Schlitz hired Kirchhoff and Rose to revamp the brewery's Palm Garden at 3rd Street and Wisconsin Avenue. Originally designed by Charles Kirchhoff in 1895, the spectacularly arched structure was one of Milwaukee's favorite restaurants and night spots. The garden was a reproduction of the beer gardens and beer halls popular in 1890s Germany, and upon its completion, it was considered to be one of the finest beer halls in the United States. Schlitz beer was the leading feature of the Palm Garden, although it was a popular place to have lunch or hear one of the city's orchestras.

The enactment of Prohibition in 1920 delivered the death blow to the Palm Garden. Rather than lose the income from this prime piece of real estate at the city's busiest intersection, the brewery commissioned Kirchhoff and Rose to convert the Palm Garden into a motion picture theater. The potted palm trees were removed and the exquisite murals were covered over. Permanent seats were fixed to the floor, the entrance of hand-carved wood was replaced, and downtown Milwaukee had another theater. With 1,250 seats in the new Garden, 2,400 in the Palace, 2,000 in the Strand, and 3,000 in the Alhambra, the once majestic 900-seat Princess was now one of the smallest of the downtown theaters, just thirteen years after it had been the largest.

Charles Kirchhoff

Competition for audiences was of cutthroat proportions, and the movie entrepreneurs had long since learned that seating the moviegoer in splendid surroundings went a long way toward assuring a full house. Often, the title of the feature was lost in the advertisements that proclaimed the glowing attributes of the theater in which it was shown.

The movement to see who could build the biggest and best picture theater had reached full steam. It would be temporarily halted in 1924 by the Saxe brothers when they astounded theater men and the general public alike with the opening of Milwaukee's first movie "palace."

Thomas Rose

CHAPTER 4

THE MOVIE PALACES

1924-1931

NOT INTENDING TO BE lost in the myriad of competitive theaters, Saxe AE in 1923 commissioned the internationally renowned architectural firm of Rapp and Rapp to design a "palace" for the motion pictures. Located at the northeast corner of 6th Street and Wisconsin Avenue, the Wisconsin theater, the twenty-eighth in the Saxe chain, opened amid a March blizzard in 1924. The theater was built as part of the Carpenter Building and had a price tag of $1,000,000. The marketing strategy and premier program for the Wisconsin were something Milwaukeeans had not yet experienced, and in spite of the weather, 2,000 people lined Wisconsin Avenue on March 28 to be part of the first audience. A seventy-five-voice choir, orchestra performance, organ duo, newsreel, Miss Wisconsin Theater beauty contest, films, and a parade from the Pfister Hotel were all part of opening day festivities.

The stunning debut of the Wisconsin theater ushered in the golden age of the "movie palace" in Milwaukee. The thing that set this new breed of theater apart from the others was

---

Opposite: The breathtaking lobby of the Wisconsin

their "theme" styling. The Wisconsin, and the Milwaukee palaces that followed it, were palaces in every sense of the word. Each one was designed with a special motif or "fantasy theme" that greatly enhanced the romantic images that Hollywood placed on the screen. The Wisconsin was similar in feeling to the Tivoli and Chicago theaters, which were designed by Rapp and Rapp for Balaban and Katz, the Chicago counterpart of Saxe AE. With its French baroque motif, grand marble staircase, and elegant chandeliers, the Wisconsin was the envy of Saxe's Milwaukee rivals. A spectacular seventy-five-foot vertical sign on the theater's exterior was the final touch, and Tom Saxe proclaimed that the huge blinking attraction could be seen for miles.

In addition to the added profits that the new palaces would bring to exhibitors, these theaters held even more significance for the patrons. The stylistic themes were designed in such a way as to mentally transport theatergoers into a land or country they might never have a chance to visit, such as Italy, the Far East, or Egypt. In addition, all customers, whether rich or poor, were treated with regal grace by a staff of highly trained ushers. A doorman, someone to take coats, and someone to assist in locating "the best remaining seats" were familiar fixtures, and going to the movies became a total experience in splendor rather than a brief, diversionary form of entertainment. In a day when traveling was a pastime reserved for the rich, the common man could pay thirty-five cents and spend three hours in a facsimile of a Viennese opera house, a French palace, or a Venetian garden. Hollywood stars became idols, and the palaces that housed their images became shrines of escape from the real world of job frustrations, money troubles, and other pressures of life. With their plush decors, ornate plasterwork, subtle lighting, and elegant themes, the movie houses had come to exceed the standards set by many of the legitimate theaters of the past.

A Saxe usher

Following the grand opening of Saxe's Wisconsin, rival exhibitors set about furiously hiring architects and soliciting financial aid in order to create theaters in a similar vein. An excellent example of combining a fantasy theater and a national craze was the Egyptian theater on North Teutonia Avenue just south of Capitol Drive. The Egyptian opened in December, 1926, with a motif that was inspired by the widespread interest generated in the United States by the excavation of King Tutankhamen's tomb in 1922. Egyptian theaters sprang up in many major cities, and Milwaukee's version was designed by local architects Peacock and Frank after the manner of a pharaoh's courtyard.

A concerted effort was made to retain as much authenticity as possible, and Peacock and Frank installed what was considered to be the most lavish combination of color and decor ever attempted in a Milwaukee picture theater. Six eighteen-foot-tall figures of simulated gold flanked the auditorium walls to represent the Colossi of Osiris, found in an Egyptian temple built around 1516 B.C. In addition, a multitude of scarabs, golden wing designs, sun discs, and other mythological symbols of ancient Egypt were incorporated into the theater's elaborate decoration. The lounge furnishings were specially designed replicas of early Egyptian pieces, and even the lighting fixtures incorporated the ancient motif, with snake patterns used as wall brackets. Attention was also paid to the small details, and pharaoh heads were present on the cast iron seat standards visible on the aisles.

The Egyptian, 3719 N. Teutonia Ave.

The Egyptian boasted a seating arrangement that allowed all 1,856 seats to have a perfect view of the stage and screen, as well as sufficient leg room for maximum comfort. The theater was a special house, too, because it was one of five Milwaukee theaters designed in the "atmospheric" style which came into prominence during the late twenties.

Atmospheric theaters were first designed in Texas by prominent architect John Eberson, who intended to give patrons the feeling that they were sitting in an open-air courtyard. The sides of the court walls rose against a blue-domed ceiling; the "sky" that twinkled with stars was actually fashioned with recessed bulbs of various colors. The atmospherics featured trees, vegetation, ivy that hung from balconies, and arcade walks. Cloud machines, hidden in the organ lofts, sent billows of vapor or a projected image, in some cases, to further enhance the illusion that one was sitting under a night sky. In addition to the Egyptian, Milwaukee's atmospheric theaters included the Avalon on South Kinnickinnic, the Zenith on North Hopkins Street, the National on National Avenue, and the Venetian.

The Venetian, located at 37th and Center Streets, was a

Opposite: Lobby of the National

The Venetian prior to opening, 1927

1,500-seat auditorium designed after an Italian garden, and it was decorated with flowers, trees, and shrubbery. An intricate electrical system operated thousands of reflectors, dimmers, and bulbs to reproduce the effect of gentle moonlight. Heavy blue-and-wine-colored draperies hung on walls that were etched with gold leaf. Two stairways ascended to the mezzanine where a beautiful promenade led to smoking lounges and restrooms. The exterior of the theater was done in buff-colored terra cotta and red brick. Additional decoration was found at each corner where a spiral molding of terra cotta was com-

The ticket booth and spacious lobby of the Garfield

plemented by a large crown of designs that recalled the splendor of the palazzos of Venice.

The theater cost over $500,000 to construct and was created by Peacock and Frank several months after completion of their work on the Egyptian. The Venetian, like many of Milwaukee's neighborhood theaters, suffered from the decay of the area surrounding it and closed in 1954. It was then used as a record store and a furniture showroom before being remodeled for its current use as a liquor store.

The Avalon theater is the only Milwaukee atmospheric that is still operating, and it is a good example of the extent to which architects went to create the outdoor illusion. The theater opened in May, 1929, and was three hard years in the making.

Milwaukee exhibitor Jack Silliman had drawn up plans in 1926 for an apartment/storefront complex that would also house his dream theater. Construction had begun on the lot at 2473 South Kinnickinnic Avenue, but Silliman ran out of money, and work on the building stopped in 1927. The steel skeleton stood idle for nearly two years while Silliman sought additional financing. Combining any and all building materials available, the theater was completed using cinder block, cream city brick, clay brick, and poured concrete. Despite Silliman's efforts to cut costs, the Avalon cost over $1,000,000 by the time it opened in 1929. One of Milwaukee's most unusual movie theaters, the Avalon appeared to be a Mediterranean courtyard, a mood enhanced by Spanish roof tiling and stucco walls. Twisted columns, common to Italian architecture, were topped off with Moorish capitals similar to those in Spain's Alhambra and Alcazar palaces. The arcade walkways and wrought iron railings combined with the rest of the decor to convince patrons that the Avalon was more than just a movie theater.

Architect Russell Barr Williamson also incorporated a blend of hanging lanterns, a proscenium arch that represented Mediterranean acanthus leaves, and two statues of the goddess Athena, patroness of Wisdom, Arts, and Civilization, above the organ lofts. The Avalon also had the unique distinction of being the first Milwaukee theater that opened with the capability to show the new synchronized sound pictures which were becoming popular after their inception in 1927.

A more modest atmospheric, called the Zenith, was the

*The Zenith on N.
Hopkins St. was the
realization of a
dream by
independent
operator Edward
Maertz*

pride and joy of owner Edward Maertz, who started in the
exhibition business by helping out at the Comfort theater,
owned by his father. The Comfort was a small neighborhood
movie house located at 24th and Hopkins Streets, about one
block from the future location of the Zenith. The Maertz family was important to the local business community, and had
interests in banking and retail investments.

In addition to his other business ventures, Fred Maertz had
built the Comfort in 1914, after gaining film experience as
manager of the Paris theater on Center Street. His sons, William and Edward, were both involved in the theater business
as independent operators, having grown up in the midst of
movies. William was an art buyer for Schuster's department
store but he managed the Colonial, and later became owner of
the Fern theater on North 3rd Street. Edward was in the business to a greater degree and began to dream about building
his own theater. As one of the founders of the Hopkins Sav-
ings and Loan Association, Edward was involved in the business transactions of many neighborhood friends. By 1925,
Edward Maertz had put together an organization of area
businessmen who joined forces to finance the building and

operation of the Zenith. The organization was called the Northwest Amusement Corporation, with Maertz as president. His brother John served as director and organizer for the theater project, but family involvement did not stop there. Maertz's daughters Frances and Helen were cashiers, and cousin Elwood Strande played the Kilgen organ, making the Zenith a very successful family-run theater. Frances acted as a cashier until 1929, earning five dollars a week. Helen then cashiered until 1936, during which time she was married. Her father hired a Pathe News cameraman to film the ceremony and showed the results during the following week's newsreel presentation.

The ownership of the Zenith passed to the Fox interests in 1939, just prior to Edward Maertz's death. The theater closed in 1954 and was converted into a church, a function that it still serves today. Unlike what had happened in many of the conversions, a good deal of the old Zenith remains, and evidence of the Spanish-style elegance can be seen on the inside as well as the outside of the building. The ornamental fish fountain and starry ceiling have long since disappeared, but the original seats are still intact, as are the proscenium arch and upper organ lofts.

The National theater, located at 2616 West National Avenue, was the first of the Milwaukee atmospherics to meet the wrecking ball. Designed in 1928 by the prominent local firm of Dick and Bauer, the National was considered by many to be the most beautiful of the atmospheric theaters when it opened that same year. Incorporated into the theater's design were balconies and ledges covered with foliage, marble pillars, plush draperies, fountains, and statues. This replica of an ancient Roman garden seated 1,388 in its heyday, but management in the 1950s and 1960s allowed the beauty of the National to deteriorate severely, and the theater was demolished in 1971 so that a housing complex could be built on the site.

With the advent of the movie palace in Milwaukee, the tug of war that had developed between chain operators and independent owners began to increase in intensity. Saxe AE, the local chain of theaters, was in direct competition with the larger Hollywood organizations, such as Warner and Fox, who wanted a bigger share of the Milwaukee market. Caught in

the middle of this power struggle were the independent theater operators who did not have the backing of a chain or unlimited capital with which to wage a battle. Consequently, the independent theater owner often found himself with second- and third-rate pictures, not being able to bid enough for the first-class films. The major studios competed furiously to establish guaranteed outlets for their pictures, with Warner Brothers, Fox, and Universal especially looking for a better foothold in Milwaukee.

Realizing the potential danger to their formidable empire of theaters, the Saxe brothers proceeded in 1926 to make a gigantic effort to undermine the activities of other chains in the city. Within a span of less than two years, Saxe AE opened five large theaters in key neighborhoods around the city. Saxe's Uptown, Plaza, Garfield, Oriental, and Tower theaters were palaces that brought the elegance of downtown movie viewing to the outlying districts. Like the independent Avalon, Egyptian, National, and Zenith, the Saxe theaters were each designed with a special theme in mind.

The Garfield at 3rd and Locust Streets was the most elegant of the five, modeled after a Viennese opera house. It was designed by Dick and Bauer, who also created the Tower at 27th and Wells Streets, and the Oriental on the corner of Farwell and North Avenues. The Tower was Mediterranean in feeling, and somewhat of a sister theater to the Oriental, but not nearly as lavish.

The Oriental was built at a cost of $1,500,000, three times as much as the Tower, and it showed. Considered by Saxe AE to be the crown jewel in its empire, the Oriental was touted on

Opposite: The National was one of five atmospheric theaters in the city. Lighting, decor, and foliage gave patrons the feeling of sitting in an open-air Roman courtyard.

Newspaper ad for opening of the Garfield

*The exotic lobby of
the Oriental*

SAXES
ORIENTAL
OPENS TONIGHT!

NORTH AT FARWELL

Opening Program

Doors Open at 6:00 With Three De Luxe Performances at

6:30 8:30 10:30

Unit No. 1
"The Voice of the Theater"

Unit No. 2
Theater Dedication

Unit No. 3
News Events

Unit No. 4
"Bernie" Cowham
at the Mammoth Organ Console

Unit No. 5
Screen Novelty
"Flying Feet"

Unit No. 6
Saxe's Oriental Theater Offers
A De Luxe Stage Presentation
"Mystic Araby"
With Billy Adair and
His Arabian Knights and
Arthur Corey—Gauthier Sisters
Eddie Willis—Novelle Brothers
Eddie Gailbreth

Unit No. 7
Feature Photoplay
Colleen Moore
in "Naughty But Nice"

Unit No. 8
Felix Cat Comedy
"Germ Mania"

Opening Program Continued Sunday and Monday

Forget the Heat!
Our $175,000 Ventilating System Chills the
Oriental to a Delightful Coolness.

Admission Prices:
Week Days, Matinees 25c, Eves. 40c
Sundays and Holidays............40c
Children, at All Times............10c

opening night in July, 1927, as the city's premier movie "temple." At Saxe AE's urging, Dick and Bauer conceived an elaborate and mystical theater that incorporated elements of East Indian, Moorish, Islamic, and Byzantine architecture to create what they called "the most beautiful and artistic temple of Oriental art to be found anywhere in America." Teakwood timbers, a trio of eight-foot chandeliers, 2,000 yards of silk, and a tiled staircase to the balcony and promenade all added to the wonder of the theater. Elaborate plaster work featured 102 elephants, as well as numerous mythological creatures. Huge murals in the lobby added to the Oriental's mystique, appearing to be scenes of the Taj Mahal and similar "neighboring" palaces.

Despite the strength of films in the latter part of the 1920s, theaters were still being designed with stages to accommodate live shows as well as motion pictures. The Oriental had a large orchestra pit, six dressing rooms, and a lighting control board that was hailed as being equal to that of the Roxy theater in New York City. Opening night at the Oriental featured a

Opposite: Opening night ad for the Oriental

Elaborate detailing inside the Oriental brought the theater's cost to $1,500,000

Saxe-O-Grams

DELUXE PROGRAM

News of Future Attractions

Published by Tower Theatre

Saxe's New Tower Theatre Welcomes All Milwaukee

Beautiful New Theatre Opens May Day

Saxe Amusement Enterprises, on this occasion, the opening of their fortieth theatre, herewith dedicate to the people of Milwaukee and surrounding community, the Tower Theatre, the newest and finest neighborhood theatre to be found any place in the country.

If, during the coming year, you and your children may have the cares of every-day life lightened with wholesome entertainment in this beautiful setting, receive inspiration, the finest music, stage presentations of art, the choice of the world's finest photoplays, their lives' work will have been rewarded.

Saxe's New Tower Theatre

Location: Twenty-seventh Street at Wells Street

stage show called "Mystic Araby," with Billy Adair and the Arabian Nights Orchestra. In addition, newsreels, a Felix the Cat cartoon, and an organ recital preceded the feature film, "Naughty but Nice," with Colleen Moore. The price of admission was forty cents and the 2,310-seat house was filled to capacity for three consecutive shows.

The other Saxe palaces were the Plaza at 13th Street and Oklahoma Avenue and the Uptown at 49th Street and North Avenue. The Uptown was designed by the firm of Rapp and Rapp, who were also involved in the designing of Saxe's Wisconsin and the new Modjeska. The Uptown, modeled after a Roman villa, was said to be very beautiful inside. Little evidence remains to prove the claims of beauty. The chandeliers have been removed and the auditorium murals have been painted over in brown. The theater stands vacant today, the last films having been shown there in 1981.

Opposite: Saxe AE handbill

The opening of the Tower breathed new life into the business district at 27th and Wells Sts.

Despite the successful operation of these five palaces, Saxe AE finally decided that it could no longer compete successfully with the Hollywood chain theaters. In December, 1927, Saxe AE sold all of its theater leases and holdings to the Wesco Corporation, also known as West Coast Theaters, Incorporated. Within six months after the sale, Wesco was purchased by the Fox Film Corporation, later known as 20th Century-Fox. At the time of the sale to Wesco, Saxe AE received $2,000,000 and Tom and John Saxe agreed that they would not re-enter the film business in Milwaukee for ten years. However, due to an unexpected turn of events, Tom Saxe would be back on top of Milwaukee's movie scene in less than five years.

Detail from the Wisconsin lobby

Three months prior to the Saxe sale to Wesco, a major upheaval shook the moving picture industry, changing it forever. The "perfection" of talking pictures — sound synchronized to film movements — had arrived. In Milwaukee, the first talking picture, "When a Man Loves," played at the Garden on Wisconsin Avenue in September, 1927.

The development of sound on film actually began as early as 1887. Thomas Edison, while working on his Kinetoscope, announced that he and his assistant William Dickson were perfecting "an instrument which would do for the eye what the phonograph does for the ear, and that by the combination of the two, all motion and sound could be recorded and reproduced simultaneously." The result of Edison's labors was the Kinetophone, an apparatus with stethoscope-like tubes that provided a reasonably synchronized, if somewhat squeaky, soundtrack to the Kinetoscope's "peep show" films. The invention was an instant but short-lived hit with the public, many of whom were leery of spending too much time in the darkened penny arcades.

Other devices to link sound and film together were the Photocinemaphone invented in 1906 and the Cameraphone of 1910, which Tom Saxe installed in the Lyric theater as a Milwaukee first. Still other methods such as the New Kinetophone in 1913, Webb's Electric Pictures in 1914, the Photokinema in 1921, and Phonofilm in 1923 came and went. As early as 1908, theaters advertised "talking pictures." The Grand theater, later remodeled into the Princess, first showed them under management of the Crawford Company, a national exhibitor of these shows. In the case of the Grand, talking pictures meant that a group of actors huddled together behind the screen and shouted out the appropriate lines in time to the action taking place on the screen. The gimmick proved to be very popular in Milwaukee, and when the Crawford people lost their lease to Saxe AE in 1909, Otto Meister began to present similar attractions at his Vaudette theater and, later on, at the Butterfly.

Experiments continued in the search for a dependable method of presenting sound with films, but it was not until 1926, and the development of the Movietone and Vitaphone systems, that sound really became an integral part of the movies. The Movietone was one method that transcribed a sound impulse that was along one edge of the film, finally providing for synchronization of dialog and action. A series of movie shorts with sync sound were produced, and then on October 6, 1927, Warner Brothers unveiled "The Jazz Singer," with a talking and singing Al Jolson. The movies were never the same again. In Milwaukee the first "talky" played at the Garden theater in September, 1927, but did not evoke the response that the Jolson film would a month later. Soon after this historic event, theaters in Milwaukee were playing pictures billed as "All Laff — All Talk" in order to let people know at a glance that a particular theater had the newest rage in movies.

Garden ad

GARDEN   DIRECTION OF L. K. BRIN

VITAPHONE

IS THRILLING MILWAUKEE!

WILL HAYS—VAN & SCHENCK—MARY LEWIS GIOVANNI MARTINELLI

and

JOHN BARRYMORE in "When a Man Loves"

COME EARLY — POPULAR PRICES

Although reluctant to face the high cost of converting their projection equipment to sound capabilities, theater owners soon discovered that people were no longer interested in seeing silent pictures. As with the nickelodeon operators of the past trying to compete with the larger photoplay houses, it was a matter of keeping up with the current whims of a fickle public. By 1928, twelve theaters in Milwaukee had been converted to sound films, and by 1929, the number had risen to fifty-eight. During the first year of the depression, twenty-one more theaters installed sound movie equipment. Those that could not afford to convert, or chose not to, were falling by the wayside. The Arcade on North 3rd Street, the Chopin on South 13th Street, the Pastime on North Avenue, the Silver City Gem on National Avenue, and the Venus on Green Bay Avenue were among the theaters that closed in 1929.

Despite the closings of a number of neighborhood houses, the late 1920s proved to be a tremendously active construction period for theaters in Milwaukee, with the key year being 1927. A total of sixteen new theaters were built in that year alone, representing 18,200 new seats at a cost of $7,000,000. These numbers for this peak year would never again be equaled. In addition, theaters costing another $2,000,000 were proposed. An example was the Arabia, a 1,500-seat palace that was to be located on North 3rd Street near Center Street. Construction was actually begun on the theater, but financing fell through and the Arabia never got past the stage of being a hole in the ground.

Marble statue from the Wisconsin

The building boom of the late 1920s also raised the seating capacity of theaters, especially the downtown houses. For example, in 1910, the average capacity for a downtown picture theater was 300. By 1920, the average house seated 1,200, and by 1930, the typical downtown picture palace had a seating capacity of over 2,000.

The flourishing construction in theater buildings also had a special significance in downtown Milwaukee for another reason. One of the theaters built during this period, the Riverside on Wisconsin Avenue, proved to be more than the other vaudeville houses on the avenue could compete with, and by 1930, the Palace and Majestic theaters were showing films in order to stay in business.

The Riverside was leased by the RKO Orpheum circuit, the top exponent of vaudeville in the country. The firm had previously booked its shows at downtown locations, including the

Palace and Majestic, but moved all of its shows to the new Riverside when it opened in 1928. The theater was designed by Kirchhoff and Rose and proved to be a much grander version of their Star theater, which was torn down in 1909 to make way for Gimbels' south annex. In the French baroque style, the Riverside featured bronze doors, marble walls and floors, gold-leaf trim, and plush wall draperies. The 2,558-seat auditorium was an elegant study in old ivory, gold, and peacock blue tones, and five grand chandeliers, which sparkled like diamond brooches, complemented the thousands of amber, blue, and red light bulbs that indirectly lit the interior with soft and subdued highlights. A gold-leaf domed ceiling loomed high overhead housing the main chandelier.

Below, vaudeville's greatest stars performed on the stage. Burns and Allen, Red Skelton, Jack Benny, Abbott and Costello, and Gene Autry all polished their acts at the Riverside theater, as did the big bands and Lucille Ball and Desi Arnaz.

Although the theater was primarily built for vaudeville, movies were shown from opening day on, usually as support for the starring act. On April 28, 1928, Ezra Buzzington's Rustic Revelers headlined the grand opening of the Riverside, and a Chester Conklin film, "The Big Noise," was also on the bill.

Just a few weeks after the Riverside opened, the Majestic theater switched to an all-movie policy, leaving the Palace to compete for the audiences that wanted vaudeville. By 1929, however, the Palace also had become an all-movie theater, leaving the Riverside as the last theater in town presenting first-rate vaudeville shows.

In 1931, as if to defy the depression that had gripped

The original Empress at 748 N. Plankinton Ave. combined risque burlesque with substandard photoplays

America's purse strings, the grandest of Milwaukee's movie palaces appeared on the scene. On May 1, the $2,500,000 Warner theater opened at 212 West Wisconsin Avenue. The Warner was part of a large office building and occupied the site where the Butterfly theater had been. The Butterfly was razed in 1930, and construction began soon after for the newest, and last, of Milwaukee's movie palaces. The theater was the most expensive, and the most elegant, that would ever be built in the city.

Opening night at the Warner theater was an extravagant affair attended by 2,500 guests. The entire evening was staged to create excitement about the movies, and especially the new theater. Milwaukee photographer Albert Kuhli was

The excitement of seeing a first-run film downtown

hired by Warner Brothers to document the inaugural festivities on film. Recently he recalled how he was told to "make a lot of noise" and explode flash powder at various intervals, even if he was not really taking a picture, just to add to the glamour and excitement of the evening.

Warner handrail

Newly arriving guests were greeted by some of the forty-four blue-clad ushers who provided curbside service and assistance into the foyer, where a classical string quartet played. The feature film of the evening was "Sit Tight," a comedy starring Joe E. Brown. The show began with the "Star Spangled Banner," which was followed by a dedicatory address by Mayor Daniel W. Hoan. Next on the bill was a newsreel, two comedy shorts, and Giovanni Martinelli, who was the leading tenor of the Metropolitan Opera Company in 1931. Just before the film, there was a performance on the massive Kimball organ and an appearance by Warner Brothers star Bebe Daniels, who introduced "Sit Tight." The film was followed by a Mickey Mouse cartoon and a fashion show. Admission to the splendor of the Warner was the most expensive in Milwaukee: fifty cents for adults on weeknights, sixty cents on Sundays. Children were fifteen cents at all times. Despite the fact that a family could eat several dinners for the price of going to the movies, the Warner proved a successful venture.

The theater was Warner's new flagship in Milwaukee and one of ten theaters under its management here. The others were the Venetian, the Egyptian, the State, the Downer, the Kosciuszko, the Granada, the Riviera, the Juneau, and the Lake.

The 2,500-seat Warner was designed by Rapp and Rapp and showcased two very distinct French architectural styles. The lobby was a three-story exercise in art deco, a popular trend in the late 1920s and early 1930s. Huge mirrors, a vaulted ceiling, silver plasterwork, marble veneer, chrome grillwork, murals, and enormous frosted glass chandeliers made the Warner lobby a breathtaking place to enter. With the mirrors reflecting the chandeliers, grand staircase, and silver ceilings, the area gave the illusion of being twice as large as it was.

Decorative touches in the hallways deviated from the art deco style to prepare the patron for the elegance of the auditorium. These included draperies and tapestries on the walls as backdrops for period furniture from late nineteenth-century mansions. Alcoves featured marble statues, fish ponds, and

Plaster relief in the Warner auditorium

Mural in the Warner balcony

drinking fountains of glazed terra cotta. The auditorium was a complete contrast to the art deco lobby, and relied on the French Renaissance style for its quiet splendor. Murals on the upper walls depicted scenes of the eighteenth-century aristocracy and were draped in velvet and lit, along with the rest of the space, by 2,000 light bulbs. Rear walls were covered with rich fabric that was interwoven with gold thread. Two large and colorful amphoras glowed from within to highlight the movements of the mythological figures on the outside.

An evening of films at the Warner was a special night out for Milwaukeeans, and to some it was even more special to work there. Gilbert Freundl, a motion picture projectionist, who was employed at nearly all of Milwaukee's theaters in his fifty-year career, remembered the significance of being asked to work at the Warner, downtown's most prestigious house. Freundl said, "When you worked at the Warner, you weren't allowed to make mistakes. They wanted only the best." He also recalls that no one just walked in and started there. "You learned your craft in one of Warner Brothers' smaller houses, like the State, or the Downer, out in the neighborhoods, and slowly worked your way to downtown. You had to prove yourself before working there."

The opening of the Warner theater in Milwaukee marked the end of the golden age of the movie palaces in this city, which lasted just seven years. The depression took its toll on the building industry in Milwaukee and across the nation, temporarily halting construction plans for theaters as well as other structures. As the last of Milwaukee's palaces to be built, the Warner still stands and operates today as a reminder and a symbol of the strength of films and theaters in the American culture.

Opposite: The Warner's huge vertical sign was one of six that adorned Wisconsin Ave.

Warner proscenium detail

CHAPTER 5

THE MOVIES PROSPER

1932-1947

DESPITE HARD TIMES, movie-going increased during the depression. In 1930, there were eighty-nine movie houses operating in Milwaukee and there would be no fewer than seventy-nine in operation for two more decades.

Promotional efforts throughout the 1930s and 1940s were designed to lure even more people to the theaters and proved to be an enormous success. Theater programs at the time always included much more than just a film. The feature presentation was the culmination of a program consisting of cartoons, newsreels, serials, organ concerts, and live stage performances.

An average Milwaukee theater changed its entire program three times a week. Without television to fill in the hours at home, it was not uncommon for people to go to the theater each time there was a program change. Frances Maertz recalls that her job at the Zenith theater meant she quickly got to know everyone in her neighborhood, because they all came to the movies so often.

Other efforts to draw the crowds made the movies much more than entertainment. They became an investment.

Opposite: Roy Rogers and Trigger in front of the Wisconsin

Theaters across the country instituted a program of giveaway nights and contests that included Dish Night, Bank Night, and Grocery Night.

On Dish Night, a woman buying a ticket would get a plate, glass dish, or bowl. Larger pieces such as serving trays or pitchers cost two admission tickets, requiring her to return to the theater more than once for a more expensive piece. After a few months of collecting, a woman could have a complete set of pink, green, blue, red, or carnival dishware, made from what we now refer to as "depression glass," all for the price of admission. With this motivation and potential saving, a housewife was inclined to bring her husband and children along each time she attended the movies, assuring a full house of satisfied customers at each show.

Bank Night proved to be another successful attraction, even though fewer people were winners in the contest. Tickets were collected over the weeks and one was drawn each Bank Night. The winner was required to be present to win. If the winner was not present, the ticket was returned to the barrel and the jackpot was increased. Sometimes five or six months would pass with no winner and the jackpot would rise as high

The Jackson, 1322 N. Jackson St.

Opposite: Milwaukee's theater listings

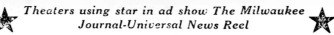

TODAY AT YOUR
NABORHOOD THEATRE

ALAMO   11th Ave. at Washington
Geo. O'Brien and Myrna Loy in "THE LAST OF THE DUANES." News "The Indians Are Coming." Laurel-Hardy Comedy.

ALLIS   West Allis   ★
All talking. Helen Twelvetrees in "HER MAN." Cartoon, Audio Review, World Events.

ASTOR   Astor and Brady Sts.
Warner Oland, Jean Arthur in "THE RETURN OF DR. FU MANCHU." Comedy, Mickey Mouse Cartoon.

ATLAS   832 Third St.
Jack Oakie in "LET'S GO NATIVE." Al Cook Comedy, Screen Song. Rin-Tin-Tin in "The Lone Defender."

AVALON   1129 Kinnickinnic Ave.
"OH, SAILOR, BEHAVE" with America's funniest clowns, Olsen and Johnson. Fables, Act, Comedy.

BURLEIGH   917 Burleigh St.   ★
Jack Oakie in "THE SOCIAL LION." Chas. Chase Comedy, Screen Song. Chap. 3, "The Indians Are Coming," mat.

CAPITOL   West Allis
All talking. Eddie Quillan in "NIGHT WORK." Novelty, Cartoon, News Events.

CLIMAX   1924 Fond du Lac Ave.
All talking. Winnie Lightner in "HOLD EVERYTHING." Laurel-Hardy Comedy, News, Cartoon.

COLONIAL   Vliet at 15th
Bessie Love in "GOOD NEWS." Comedy, News, Novelty.

COMET   34th and North Ave.
"WITH BYRD AT THE SOUTH POLE." Weekly, Comedy. Admission 10c before 7 p. m.

DOWNER   Downer Ave. and Belleview
Gloria Swanson in "WHAT A WIDOW." Milton C. Work in "A Bridge Lesson."

EGYPTIAN   20th & Teutonia Ave.
Warner Bros. Present Frank Fay in "MATRIMONIAL BED." Adults 25c.

ELITE   1364 Green Bay Ave.   ★
"Manslaughter" with Claudette Colbert. Review, Comedy, Serial. Thurs. night, radio free. Wed., Thurs., "Happy Days."

GEM   931 S. Fifth St.
"GOLDEN CALF" with Jack Mulhall and Sue Carol. Comedy, "The Indians Are Coming."

GRACE   1207 National Ave.
"Common Clay" shown 7.30 to 9 p. m. "Good Intentions" added feature. This ad and 1 paid adult admits 2 adults tonight.

GRANADA   1125 W. Mitchell St.
Stanley Smith and Ginger Rogers in "QUEEN HIGH." N. Y. paid $5.50 to see this stage show.

GRAND   1171 Holton St.   ★
John Barrymore and Joan Bennett in "MOBY DICK." Comedy, Fables, Sportlight.

HOLLYWOOD   1730 Green Bay Ave.
Grant Withers and Sue Carol in "DANCING SWEETIES." Comedy, Review, Cartoon.

JACKSON   676 Jackson St.
Double feature program. H. B. Warner in "WILD COMPANY." Benny Rubin in "HOT CURVES."

JUNEAU   611 W. Mitchell St.   ★
Bebe Daniels in "LOVE COMES ALONG." Free dresserware to the ladies.

LAKE   Delaware and Rusk Aves.   ★
"THE SOCIAL LION" with Jack Oakie. Harry Langdon Comedy, "Big Kick." Adults 25c.

LAYTON PARK   Layton Blvd. and Lincoln
Comedy drama, "The Dude Wrangler." This ad and 1 paid adult admits 2 adults tonight. News, Comedy.

LEXINGTON   17th & Center Sts.
Richard Barthelmess in "The Dawn Patrol." Laurel-Hardy in "Brats." News, Cartoon, "The Indians Are Coming."

LIBERTY   2619 Vliet St.
All talking. Bargain night. All seats 10c. Rex Lease and Benny Rubin in "SUNNY SKIES." Comedy, News, Cartoon.

LYRIC   3804 Vliet St.
Greta Garbo in "ROMANCE." Fables, Comedy, Western Feature.

MILWAUKEE   1082 Teutonia Ave.
Richard Dix in "SHOOTING STRAIGHT." Matinee daily at 2 o'clock.

MIRAMAR   688 Oakland Ave.
Constance Bennett in "COMMON CLAY." "Lone Defender," News, Felix Cat.

MIRTH   2653 Kinnickinnic Ave.
Bebe Daniels in "Lawful Larceny." "The Indians Are Coming." Comedy, News. 15c to 7 p. m. 25c after; child. 10c.

NATIONAL   1030 National Ave.
Request night. Douglas Fairbanks, Jr., in "WAY OF ALL MEN." Novelties, Comedy.

PARKWAY   35th & Lisbon Ave.
Clara Bow in "HER WEDDING NIGHT." Mickey Mouse Cartoon. Laurel-Hardy Comedy, "Below Zero." 15c to 7 p. m.

PASTIME   2212 W. Greenfield Ave.
"Song of Kentucky." "Mexicali Rose." Jade dresserware free to the ladies. Save coupons for Xmas gifts.

PEARL   1700 S. 19th St.
John McCormack in "SONG O' MY HEART." This ad and 1 paid adult admits 2 adults tonight.

PEERLESS   Center & Holton Sts.
Richard Arlen, Jack Holt, Fay Wray in "THE BORDER LEGION." Fables, News, Comedy.

PLAZA   3067 S. 13th St.
"GOLDEN DAWN." Comedy, News, Organ. 15c before 7 p. m., kiddies 10c.

RADIO   2505 Fond du Lac Ave.
All talking. Richard Barthelmess in "THE DAWN PATROL." Comedy, News, Cartoon. 6:30 to 7 p. m. 10c.

RAINBOW   2718 Lisbon Ave.
All talking. Constance Bennett and Lew Ayres in "COMMON CLAY." Comedy, News, Fables.

RITZ   North Milwaukee
Conrad Nagel in "A LADY SURRENDERS." Talking Comedy, News. Movie Star Contest.

RIVIERA   1005 W. Lincoln Ave.   ★
George O'Brien in "THE LAST OF THE DUANES." Laurel-Hardy in "Below Zero."

SAVOY   27th and Center Sts.
Bebe Daniels in "LAWFUL LARCENY." "The Indians Are Coming." Comedy, News. Early price 15c, 6:30 to 7 p. m.

SHOREWOOD   4337 N. Oakland Ave.
All talking. Maurice Chevalier in "PLAYBOY OF PARIS." Dec. 18-20. Eddie Cantor in "Whoopee."

STATE   State and 27th Sts.   ★
"THE GIRL OF THE GOLDEN WEST" with the incomparable Ann Harding and James Rennie.

STUDIO   Ogden Ave. & Marshall St.
"BROADWAY SCANDALS" with Sally O'Neil, Jack Egan, Carmel Myers.

TIVOLI   3302 North Ave.
A comedy riot. Jack Mulhall in "THE FALL GUY." 6:30 to 7 p. m., all seats 10c.

VENETIAN   37th and Center Sts.   ★
Conrad Nagel in "A LADY SURRENDERS," a wonderful picture. Movietone Act, News.

VIOLET   2430 Vliet St.
"THREE FACES EAST" with Constance Bennett, Eric von Stroheim. "The Indians Are Coming." Comedy, Fables.

ZENITH   25th and Hopkins Sts.
Joan Crawford in "OUR BLUSHING BRIDES." News, Mickey Mouse, Screen Act, Comedy.

Fox-Wisconsin employees at a company picnic

as $1,000. Although Bank Night proved to be the best drawing card for the theaters during the depression years, a Wisconsin law passed in the early 1940s outlawed the contests.

With attendance high and the movie theaters well established, exhibition was becoming an extremely sophisticated and slick business. The competition became fierce between the studios and the independent theater owners.

The rift between the independents and the chains had existed for many years. As early as 1909, the trade publication *Motion Picture World* ran an appeal to the independent owners to join together "in a united effort to save themselves from the impending actions of the motion picture patent companies, just now starting on its (sic) career of monopoly and extortion." The appeal asked independent operators to create a fund to be used for defense against patent companies which were intimidating exhibitors by threatening to close their houses unless those businessmen signed a license agreement to show the chains' films. The appeal concluded by saying, "Stop, think, and be sure that the hour for united action is at hand and our call for support is opportune and necessary for your salvation."

This zest for independent exhibition survived, and by the late 1930s there existed a powerful national alliance of independent theater owners. These owners banded together in mutual support against the Hollywood chains that were fast becoming more and more powerful.

Edward Maertz was president of the Independent Theater Owners Protective Association in 1939 when state government proposed a two-dollar-and-fifty-cent tax on all motion picture films shown in Wisconsin. In protest, he addressed a Senate Committee in Madison and, by stating the independents' position, eloquently pointed out the importance of the motion picture to America's well-being. Although the tax was

The Mirth on S. Kinnickinnic Ave.

directed at film distributors, license agreements between distributors and exhibitors stated that any such tax or fee would be paid by the exhibitor. The tax, according to Maertz, would crush the motion picture industry.

To bolster his protest, he submitted that:

> *Motion pictures are a necessity, not a luxury – they should be neither crippled nor destroyed. Motion pictures furnish wholesome entertainment for the great mass of our citizens, for the thousands of farmers and workers of Wisconsin, at a price within reach of everyone. In fact, motion pictures have been called the "poor man's entertainment." In these times of discouragement, due to the strenuous period through which we are now passing because of the continued depression, it is necessary to one's morale – yes, even to one's health and sanity – to forget for a few hours, to relax and enjoy a good comedy, to laugh and forget one's worries, to see an inspiring drama, and to give one courage. Entertainment and relaxation are as necessary to the mental well-being as food is necessary to the body. All of this gives one the strength to carry on and, more often, gives one a new perspective to work.*

Edward Maertz

Opposite: The Plaza on S. Thirteenth St.

Maertz then cited an example in Chicago in 1927, when a tax program caused the closing of theaters. Those wishing to attend the movies roamed the streets, threatening civic peace and order. Concluding, Maertz pleaded, "If this was the situation in Chicago in 1927, it does not take much imagination to know what would happen today if the theaters closed in Wisconsin. We earnestly request your consideration of this fact."

The work that Edward Maertz did on behalf of the independent theater owners was greatly respected among his contemporaries. The members of the association needed leaders such as Maertz to direct their noble alliance in the fight against the chain operators, unfair taxation, and other problems of the day.

The most promising member of the league in the 1930s and 1940s was Ben Marcus. Marcus, a Polish immigrant, began in the theater business via his sales position with a newspaper in Minneapolis. By selling ads to motion picture theaters, he developed a relationship with the theater managers, as well as a taste for the business.

Marcus purchased his first movie theater, the Campus, in

Ben Marcus, circa 1935

Ripon, Wisconsin, in 1935. In 1940, he purchased his first Milwaukee property, the Tosa, on West North Avenue. And by the end of 1941, he had expanded his state-wide holdings through theaters in Sparta, Reedsburg, Oshkosh, Tomah, Neenah, and Appleton.

Marcus used two principles to build his state-wide circuit, insuring its success in spite of the pressure from the huge chains. These were: putting all the theaters' profits back into the business and operating all theaters with the highest possible standards. By implementing these principles and surviving the most difficult years in the movie business, he went on to become the leading film exhibitor in Wisconsin, controlling more than 100 movie screens in the state as well as a chain of hotels, motels, and restaurants throughout the Midwest.

The power of the chain operators was given a considerable shot in the arm when the Saxe brothers sold their exhibition rights in 1927. After 20th Century-Fox's purchase of the Saxe holdings, its influence steadily increased in Wisconsin, and especially in Milwaukee. By 1930, the company controlled exhibition rights in sixty theaters, over half of them in Milwaukee. But in 1931, having overextended themselves, the Fox people found that their business was failing and they

Ben Marcus with Charlton Heston

Vaudeville and burlesque shows fell onto hard times after the inception of talking pictures, and in order to survive, many of the theaters began to present increasingly risque comedy shows and female revues. In Milwaukee, no burlesque impresario ever came close to competing with Charlie Fox, the fast-talking, cane-twirling manager of the Gayety. Fox cut a legendary figure on N. Third St. as he barked, "Seven, count 'em, seven beauties on the inside," while hooking the arms of passersby with his cane. During the show, Fox went up the aisles hawking peanuts and candy, promising a prize in every box. No one ever recalled getting a prize. By the mid-1940s Fox was booking strippers Gypsy Rose Lee, Rose La Rose, and Lili St. Cyr. Between shows he would chase the customers out of the theater by showing the worst films he could find. Fox died in 1963 while trying to engineer the comeback of Milwaukee's golden age of burlesque.

were forced to sell back what they had gained. Tom Saxe bought back the rights to all of his old Milwaukee theaters and allied himself with Warner Brothers, which had been Fox's stiffest competitor. The Warner/Saxe alliance continued in Milwaukee until Saxe's death in 1938.

Due to a hierarchical structure established by those most powerful in the business, the independent operators, despite their numbers, had little hope of ever acquiring first-run films for their theaters. All theaters had been broken down into classifications, ranging from first-run houses, showing the newest and best of the studios' output, to twelfth-run houses. With the major studios controlling all of the first- and second-run theaters in the city, the independents were forced into

The Varsity, 1326 W. Wisconsin Ave.

A rare interior view of the Murray

being third- to twelfth-run houses. The lowest theaters on the ladder would not receive a picture until ninety-one days after it had premiered in the city.

The only hope the independents had for negotiating for better films was to "block book," requiring them to order a block of films, most of which were poor quality and some of which had not even been produced, in order to receive a first-run film. This method would often tie up a theater's exhibition schedule for an entire year, and it was obviously much more advantageous to the studio than to the independent exhibitor. Although it was this sort of policy that had helped the chains to become as influential and powerful as they were, it would hurt more in the long run, since it brought about a stream of anti-trust legislation against them.

As the 1930s neared a close, the federal government decreed that the motion picture studios were in violation of

The Layton, 2275 S. Layton Blvd.

anti-monopoly laws by controlling the production, distribution, and exhibition of their own product. The result of this was a Supreme Court decision that ordered the studios to sell their theaters, thus divorcing themselves from the exhibition end of the motion picture business. However, lengthy litigation held up the enforcement of the ruling, and many of the studios were able to forestall the inevitable until almost 1950.

In Milwaukee these practices resulted in a precedent-setting lawsuit instigated by the Towne theater, against virtually every major film distributing chain. Despite the fact that the Towne was one of the largest downtown theaters, it was never able to obtain first-run films because of its independent status. After a drawn-out court battle, the U.S. Court of Appeals ruled that the owners of the Towne were indeed being discriminated against, and the Film Board of Trade was ordered to give the Towne first-run status.

This hard-fought victory for the independent theater owners came just in time — at the height of movie popularity. Theater attendance reached its peak in 1946, with major film studios pumping out films in quantities that would never again be equaled.

The "star system" was in full swing, with viewers turning out to watch Humphrey Bogart and Lauren Bacall, James Stewart, Joan Crawford, Katharine Hepburn and Spencer Tracy, and hundreds of other stars. The newsreels, a long-time staple in movie programming, continued to furnish the

Community theaters were tremendous supporters of the United States war effort. Various promotions were held to raise needed funds and to increase the public's awareness of its obligation to servicemen.

news of the day in America's movie theaters. The theater's importance as a news source became frighteningly evident when, in 1941, Japan bombed the American naval base at Pearl Harbor. The Avalon and Venetian theaters interrupted their showing of "Here Comes Mr. Jordan" to announce the disaster. "Hold That Ghost," with Abbott and Costello, was stopped at the Climax, Zenith, and Tivoli theaters; and at the Granada, "International Squadron," with Ronald Reagan, was halted to bring the news to the theater audience. Later, the Riverside theater played its part as a news source by announcing, over its public address system to all of downtown Milwaukee, that President Roosevelt had declared war on Japan.

The Princess in the 1940s

The government found movie theaters to be a tremendous rallying point for support of the war effort. Movie stars filmed spots that were shown in the theaters, pledging their support and asking members of the audience to buy war bonds. The stars would plead, "Think of our boys overseas, fighting and dying to preserve our way of life. Surely you can spare a few dollars to help them!" Theaters across the country sold war bonds and displayed posters in support of United States efforts overseas.

One of Milwaukee's most innovative fundraisers was Arnold Brumm, manager of the Ritz theater on Villard Avenue. Brumm began in the business as a child, helping his father Michael sweep sawdust from his north side nickelodeon, the Princess, on opening day. During the summers, when business declined, the Brumm family would travel to outlying areas with a portable generator and a movie projector, bringing the movies to the farmers or businessmen in small towns without movie theaters. The show was done on a weekly circuit, with posters left behind to advertise the next week's feature.

When Michael Brumm opened the Ritz theater in 1926, he no longer operated the traveling shows and settled into more routine business operations. Arnold became the assistant

Ritz billboard

The remodeled Comet

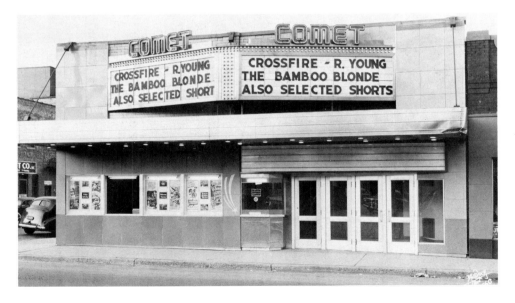

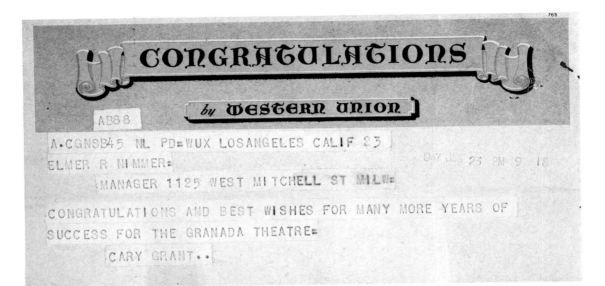

CONGRATULATIONS

by WESTERN UNION

AB8-8

A·CGNSB45 NL PD=WUX LOSANGELES CALIF 23

ELMER R NIMMER=

MANAGER 1125 WEST MITCHELL ST MILW=

CONGRATULATIONS AND BEST WISHES FOR MANY MORE YEARS OF

SUCCESS FOR THE GRANADA THEATRE=

CARY GRANT··

1947 JUL 23 PM 9 18

Cary Grant's congratulatory telegram to the Granada's manager

manager of the theater after graduating from high school and eventually took over the business altogether.

Although he had always been known for his innovative advertising techniques, such as displaying movie posters upside down to attract attention, Brumm pulled off his most successful stunt when promoting the sale of war bonds. Coming up short on the bond sale quota set for his theater, Brumm decided to climb to the top of the Ritz theater's five-story chimney and stay there until his quota was met. A huge sign on the theater's chimney screamed, "BUY ME DOWN WITH BONDS." He climbed up to his precarious perch armed only with a telephone at 3:00 p.m. on a Saturday afternoon in 1944. He stayed at his post for twenty-four hours, and when bond sales were tallied on Monday morning, Brumm found that his efforts had not only enabled the theater to meet its quota, but to double it!

After the release of "Gone With the Wind" in 1939, and a contract that required the selling of Atlanta-based Coca-Cola during the intermission, fans began to see concession stands springing up in their neighborhood theaters. The phenomenon began with ushers bringing drinks down the aisles on trays and evolved into the elaborate setup we know today, with the sale of popcorn, soft drinks, candy, and sometimes even hot

Refreshment stands ranged from the Layton's tiny operation to the Uptown's sophisticated one

Representation:

TOMMY WONDER AND DON DELLAIR

420 MADISON AVENUE
NEW YORK, N. Y. 10017

(212) 752-3210

Hildegarde, the internationally famous cabaret singer, got her start as a professional musician in the silent movie theaters of Milwaukee. While still in high school, she was hired by the Lyric theater on W. Vliet St. to play the organ for Saturday and Sunday matinees. In 1925, just two years later, Hildegarde made her debut on the keyboards at the Alhambra theater. She recalled that "it was a thrilling week for me." Before leaving Milwaukee to join a traveling vaudeville show, Hildegarde also played the organ at the Wisconsin theater, and was the only woman musician in the 12-piece Merrill theater house orchestra.

*Milwaukee's first
newsreel theater*

dogs. Only a few theaters had installed concession stands in the early 1940s. Most waited until later in the decade and the early 1950s when movie attendance began to fall.

The great victory the independents had won over the chain operators was short-lived, since the decline of movie attendance was just over the horizon. The new concession stand would eventually become a necessity, rather than a novelty, as more and more theaters began to rely on it as a major source of revenue.

In 1947, the Telenews theater opened on Wisconsin Avenue. This theater was unique because it served as a news source, showing newsreels and sponsoring radio broadcasts. The theater also proved to be an indicator of things to come, when it installed the new "television" in its lobby to feature broadcasts from WTMJ, Milwaukee's first television station. Although the new television medium did not at first appear to be a threat to the movies, in the early 1950s its quality improved and its price came down, so that more and more people were able to buy television sets.

CHAPTER 6

THE DECLINING YEARS

1948-Present

I N 1950 THERE WERE eighty movie theaters in Milwaukee. Of those, only two, the Telenews and the Fox Bay, had been built after World War II. By 1960, the number of operating theaters had been cut almost in half: there were forty-five. Unquestionably, the main reason for the rapid demise of the theaters was the advent and subsequent availability of television.

By the end of the 1950s, nearly every family in America could afford a television set, and almost every household owned one. Another major reason for the decline of theater attendance was the physical deterioration of many of the structures. When the studios were forced by law to divest themselves of their theater interests, systematic upkeep on the buildings stopped in almost all cases. Their new owners were concerned mainly with profit, and therefore spent the minimum on maintenance and repairs. Consequently, the once-grand theaters began to fall into a state of disrepair. And because of television, people were now able to stay at home for their entertainment. The golden age of the movie theater was dead from this point on as the whole process began to

Opposite: The end of an era

The Strand, built in 1915, was completely remodeled by the 1950s, giving the old photoplay house a contemporary appearance

move in a vicious circle. The movie studios began to feel the crunch and made a concerted effort to lure people out of their living rooms and back into the theaters with such gimmicks as 3-D movies and Cinerama.

For a short time, 3-D, a new technique of double projection that produced a three-dimensional image on the screen, had patrons swarming to the theaters. The first feature film released in 3-D was called "Bwana Devil," and it played in Milwaukee in 1953 simultaneously at two downtown theaters, the Palace and the Wisconsin, directly across the street from each other. The waiting lines were around the block at each theater. The popularity of 3-D was short-lived, however, as people soon tired of the gimmick, as well as the headaches and nausea that were caused by careless projection.

Cinerama, which widened the image of the motion picture, was a more subtle version of three-dimensional viewing. The overly wide picture increased the quality of viewing, but only succeeded on an intermittent basis. Viewers were becoming more sophisticated and began to expect a high standard for image quality in the films they saw. Cinerama soon became nothing more than one of the many technical improvements

Cary Grant at Milwaukee's Paramount film exchange

All evidence of the Princess theater's former elegance was gone by the time it became an adult cinema

they had come to expect. Cinerama also brought the problem of installing larger screens in theaters, to accommodate the new image size. In many houses the once elegant and elaborate prosceniums were being hidden behind large cineramic screens.

Despite the industry's concerted effort to improve film quality and keep audiences in the theaters, the 1950s proved to be disastrous for Milwaukee's exhibitors. In 1954, the Davidson theater kept a long-awaited date with the wrecking ball, while the once breathtaking Venetian closed, along with several other neighborhood theaters.

The following year saw Edward Maertz's Zenith theater converted into a religious building. The Department of Theater Inspection concluded that the staggering total of 13,594 theater seats were lost during the years 1954 to 1956 due to closings or razings.

By 1960, the Alhambra had closed for good. The last films shown were the low-quality thrillers, "H-Men" and "The Woman Eaters." With low-grade horror as its mainstay through the 1950s, it had become inevitable that the Alhambra was on its last legs. The sixty-four-year-old theater was torn down soon after its closing.

Other downtown theaters which had been virtually abandoned by patrons since the late 1950s found that the high cost of operation, coupled with poor attendance, was more than they could withstand. In addition, there was new competition coming from the recent construction of the suburban movie houses such as the Mayfair, Southgate, and Capitol Court

The Mt. Pilgrim Baptist Church at 2202 W. Center St. was once the Paris

theaters. These theaters were all located near another phenomenon of the 1960s, the shopping center. In an attempt to cut costs and offer more variety on the screen, the once mighty Wisconsin theater, the flagship of the Saxe fleet, was remodeled into an upstairs and downstairs set of theaters, losing much of the decor in the process.

Throughout the 1960s, the shopping center theaters found enough of an audience to sustain themselves, but back in the city, the older houses were closing faster than ever. Due to

John Freuler remodeled the old Atlas on N. Third St. into the Century

The Regal, a long-time resident of W. Walnut St., closed permanently in 1958

rapidly disintegrating neighborhoods and suburban flight, theaters such as the Garfield, Egyptian, Century, Liberty, Rainbow, National, and Granada all had closed by 1969.

The following year saw another trend-setting theater, the triplex, appear at 76th Street and Mill Road. This was the first local use of the concept incorporating three separate screens housed under one roof. Other triple theaters began to appear in shopping complexes across the city, most notably on North and South 76th Streets, as part of the Northridge and Southridge shopping malls. The success of this led Northridge to add three additional screens, bringing the total to six.

These tiny unadorned units represented a new attitude in movie going. Physically, they were very similar to the early nickelodeon theaters, with a long, narrow, box-like auditorium, small screens, absence of decor, and seating for about 300. Architecturally they were a far cry from the theater temples of the 1920s that seated 2,000.

The year 1973 saw the former Warner theater meeting the same fate as the Wisconsin theater. It became the Centre 1 and 2, losing much of its majesty in the process, despite the careful twinning done by the owners. The Tower theater was closed and annexed to Family Hospital for storage purposes.

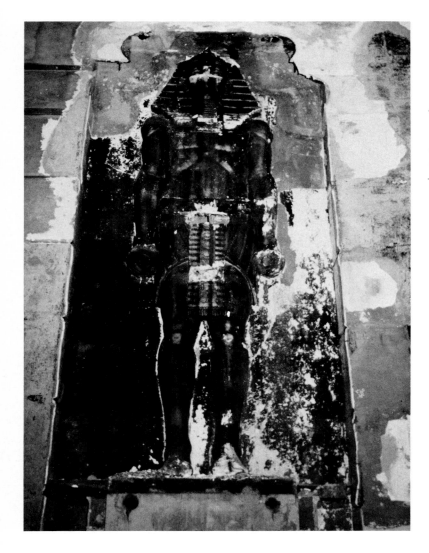

   In 1979, the Strand and Towne theaters were torn down to make room for parking lots. Later the Esquire fell to the wrecking ball prior to the erection of the new federal building plaza. The summer of 1983 saw the razing of the decaying Apollo theater at Center Street and Teutonia Avenue. And in January, 1984, the once mystical Egyptian theater was condemned and demolished. City planners were able to remove

In March, 1986, workers removed the valuable marble statue from the former Wisconsin as the building was readied for demolition

the mosaic ticket booth before the theater went down, thus preserving at least one memory of the movie palace era.

In August, 1984, demolition began on the historic Princess theater at 738 North Third Street. By far the city's oldest operating movie house, the theater was purchased by the Milwaukee Redevelopment Authority and razed at the age of eighty. The Princess was the last remaining survivor of the once-proud theater row that existed on North 3rd Street in the block between Wells Street and Wisconsin Avenue. The White House, Magnet, Vaudette, American, and Empress were some of the theaters that once provided entertainment there.

Most recently, the Carpenter Building, housing the former Wisconsin theater at Sixth Street and Wisconsin Avenue, was purchased for demolition. The theater, known since 1963 as the Cinemas 1 and 2, closed its doors for the last time in October, 1985. In its final months, the Cinemas operated on a weekend-only basis with films consisting of cheap horror and

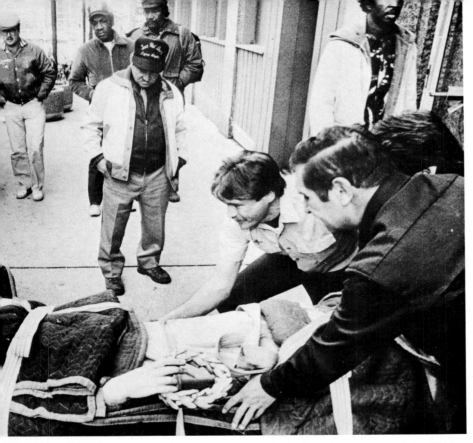

exploitation titles. By June, 1986, the theater and building were scheduled for a summer demolition.

Today, vacant lots, like missing teeth, designate where the movie theaters once reigned. Churches, warehouses, grocery stores, and nightspots occupy the buildings that housed the altars of amusement in the years between 1910 and 1950.

The year 1930 was a peak one for the theater business in Milwaukee, with eighty-nine theaters showing films. Of those, only seven are still in operation today. These are the Downer, Grand Cinemas 1 and 2 (Warner), Modjeska, Avalon, Paradise, Oriental, and Riverside theaters.

But even more apparent than the operating theaters are the vacant lots and boarded-up empty hulks that decay from the inside out. Theaters such as the Elite, Uptown, and Lincoln now stand silent, much the same as the Egyptian did before its demise. These and many other buildings loom against the sky as testaments to the days when Milwaukee was in love with the movies.

MILWAUKEE'S MOVIE THEATERS

The following information is a listing of Milwaukee movie theaters, cross-indexed by all known names. The original name of the theater contains additional specifics such as the street address, dates of operation, architect (if known), seating capacity, make of organ (if known), and the current status of the building.

ABBY (*See Greenfield*)
2212 West Greenfield Avenue

ACADEMY OF MUSIC
(*Imperial, Lyceum, Shubert*)
623 North Milwaukee Street
1866-1923
Architect: Edward Townsend Mix
Seating: 1,680
Razed

ACE (*See NATIONAL*)
905 South 5th Street

AETNA (*See ROYAL*)
3000 North 12th Street

AIRDOME (*See UNION ELECTRIC*)
2161 South Kinnickinnic Avenue

AIRDOME²
1502 South 2nd Street
1911-1912
Razed

AIRWAY
4001 South Howell Avenue
1949-1967
Architects: Peacock & Belongia
Seating: 550
Razed

ALAMO (*See IDLE HOUR*)
1037 South 16th Street

ALHAMBRA
334 West Wisconsin Avenue
1896-1960
Architect: Charles Kirchhoff
Seating: 2,500
Organ: 2/6 Wurlitzer
Razed

ALLIS
7224 West Greenfield Avenue
1912-1952
Architect: John Ganser
Seating: 850
Organ: Barton
Lighting fixture store

AMERICAN
742 North 3rd Street
1910-1924
Architects: Kirchhoff & Rose
Seating: 700
Razed

AMERICAN² (*See IRIS*)
2459 West Fond du Lac Avenue

APOLLO
2754 North Teutonia Avenue
1911-1921
Razed

APOLLO² (*See MILWAUKEE*)
2754 North Teutonia Avenue

ARABIA
2700 North 3rd Street
1926
Architects: Peacock & Frank
Seating: 1,600
Began construction; never completed

ARAGON (*See AVENUE*)
2311 South Howell Avenue

ARCADE
2305 North 3rd Street
194-1929
Architect: Peter Christiansen
Seating: 697
Razed

ARMORY HALL
(*Imperial*[2])
2674 North Richards Street
1910-1913
Seating: 683
Razed

ASTOR
1696 North Astor Street
1914-1952
Architect: Hugo Miller
Seating: 752
Drug store

ATLANTIC (*See WHITE HOUSE*)
739 North 3rd Street

ATLAS
(*Century*)
2342 North 3rd Street
1910-1966
Seating: 890
Razed

AURORA
3002 North 3rd Street
1911-1920
Architect: John Roth, Jr.
Seating: 598
Office building

AVALON
(*Garden*[3])
2473 South Kinnickinnic Avenue
1929-Present
Architect: Russell Barr Williamson
Seating: 1,637
Organ: 3/12 Wurli-Bart
Operating theater

AVENUE
(Pix, Aragon)
2311 South Howell Avenue
1910-1961
Architect: Stanley Kadow
Seating: 481
Razed

BADGER *(See UNION ELECTRIC)*
2161 South Kinnickinnic Avenue

BAY *(See LAKE)*
2893 South Delaware Avenue

BELL
(Lyceum, Iris², Roosevelt)
1402 West North Avenue
1911-1965
Architect: Jacob Jacobi
Seating: 797
Food store

BERGMANN
926 Milwaukee Avenue
1911-1915
Seating: 150
Drug store

BIJOU
(*Gayety²*, *Garrick²*)
631 North 2nd Street
1890-1931
Architect: Oscar Cobb
Seating: 1,800
Razed

BOULEVARD
(*Layton, Layton Park*)
2275 South Layton Boulevard
1911-1971
Seating: 600
Razed

BURLEIGH
925 West Burleigh Street
1915-1957
Architect: Arthur Swager
Seating: 828
Organ: 2/6 Barton
Church

BUTTERFLY
212 West Wisconsin Avenue
1911-1930
Architect: August Willmanns
Seating: 1,500
Organ: 3 manual, make unknown
Razed

CAMEO (*See COMMUNITY*)
6416 West Greenfield Avenue

CAPITOL
7239 West Greenfield Avenue
1923-1967
Architect: Robert Messmer
Seating: 750
Organ: Kilgen
Office building

CAPITOL[2] *(See MILWAUKEE)*
2754 North Teutonia Avenue

CASINO
(Olympic)
704 West Walnut Street
1909-1917
Architect: John Menge, Jr.
Seating: 274
Razed

CASTLE *(See IRIS)*
2459 West Fond du Lac Avenue

CENTRAL
(Pulaski, Pola Negri, Popularity, Midget, 8th Street Theater, Delta)
1662 South 8th Street
1910-1953
Architect: Stanley Kadow
Seating: 250
Offices/flats

CENTRE *(See WARNER)*
212 West Wisconsin Avenue

CHOPIN
(8th Avenue Theater, Eagle[2])
2922 South 13th Street
1916-1929
Seating: 483
Workshop

CINEMAS 1 and 2 *(See WISCONSIN)*
530 West Wisconsin Avenue

CLIMAX
1954 West Fond du Lac Avenue
1911-1957
Architects: Duggan & Huff
Seating: 1,000
Razed

COLISEUM
(*Empire*[2], *White House*[3], *Cudahy*)
4763 South Packard Avenue
1909-1963
Seating: 400
Razed

COLONIAL
(*Palace, Player*)
1023 Milwaukee Avenue
1910-1914
Seating: 450
Razed

COLONIAL[2]
7214 West Greenfield Avenue
1910-1912
Seating: 600
Razed

COLONIAL[3]
1514 West Vliet Street
1914-1926
Architects: Kirchhoff & Rose
Seating: 800
Remodeled into Colonial[4]

COLONIAL[4]
1514 West Vliet Street
1926-1964
Architects: Dick & Bauer
Seating: 1,500
Organ: 3/10 Barton
Razed

COLUMBIA (*See WEST SIDE TURN HALL*)
1023 West Walnut Street

COMET
3324 West North Avenue
1910-1956
Seating: 642
Nightclub

COMFORT
2440 West Hopkins Street
1914-1934
Seating: 600
Tavern

COMIQUE
2246 South Kinnickinnic Avenue
1905-1909
Architect: Nicholas Dornbach
Seating: 200
Liquor store

COMMUNITY
(*Cameo*)
6416 West Greenfield Avenue
1916-1927
Architect: Charles Lesser
Seating: 600
Tavern

CORONET (*See HOLLYWOOD*)
3832 North Green Bay Avenue

CROWN
2514 North Teutonia Avenue
1909-1911
Seating: 200
Razed

COZY (*See VAUDETTE²*)
1036 East Brady Street

COZY² (*See WAUWATOSA THEATER DELIGHT*)
7208 West State Street

The Crystal was converted from a theater to a nightclub.

CRYSTAL
726 North 3rd Street
1903-1907
Architects: Leiser & Holst
Remodeled into Crystal[2]

CRYSTAL[2]
726 North 3rd Street
1907-1929
Architects: Kirchhoff & Rose
Seating: 1,032
Razed

CUDAHY (*See COLISEUM*)
4763 South Packard Avenue

DAVIDSON
625 North 3rd Street
1890-1954
Architects: Burnham & Root
Seating: 1,200
Razed

DELTA *(See CENTRAL)*
1662 South 8th Street

DOWNER
2589 North Downer Avenue
1915-Present
Architect: Martin Tullgren
Seating: 940
Organ: 2/8 Wurlitzer
Operating as theater

EAGLE
1546 North 12th Street
1909-1912
Seating: 209
Razed

EAGLE² *(See CHOPIN)*
2922 South 13th Street

EAST *(See MURRAY)*
2342 North Murray Avenue

EGYPTIAN
3719 North Teutonia Avenue
1926-1967
Architects: Peacock & Frank
Seating: 1,419
Organ: 2/8 Barton
Razed

8TH AVENUE THEATER *(See CHOPIN)*
2922 South 13th Street

8TH STREET THEATER *(See CENTRAL)*
1662 South 8th Street

ELECTRIC JOY
1117 Milwaukee Avenue
1907-1908
Seating: 400
Tavern

ELITE
(Roxy, Mars)
3240 North Green Bay Avenue
1910-1952
Architect: Edward Kozick
Seating: 700
Warehouse

EMBASSY *(See EMPRESS)*
748 North Plankinton Avenue

EMPIRE
(Granada)
1125 West Mitchell Street
1906-1968
Architect: Anton Dohmen
Seating: 900
Organ: Barton
Razed

EMPIRE² *(See COLISEUM)*
4763 South Packard Avenue

EMPORIUM
(Imperial 5¢ Theater)
626 West Mitchell Street
1906-1908
Seating: 175
Razed

EMPRESS
(Embassy)
748 North Plankinton Avenue
1909-1929
Seating: 1,100
Razed

EMPRESS² *(See NEW STAR)*
755 North 3rd Street

ESQUIRE *(See TELENEWS)*
310 West Wisconsin Avenue

FOX BAY
334 East Silver Spring Drive
1950-Present
Architects: Ebling, Plunkett, & Keymar
Seating: 916
Operating as theater

FERN
2556 North 3rd Street
1911-1955
Architect: Charles Smith
Seating: 580
Church

FOND DU LAC ELECTRIC
(See TRINZ ELECTRIC THEATER[2])
1465 West Fond du Lac Avenue

FRANKLIN *(See LEXINGTON)*
1706 West Center Street

GARDEN
(Little, Newsreel)
235 West Wisconsin Avenue
1921-1955
Architects: Kirchhoff & Rose
Seating: 1,250
Organ: 2/5 Wurlitzer
Razed

GARDEN[2] *(See RIALTO[2])*
1005 Milwaukee Avenue

GARDEN[3] *(See AVALON)*
2473 South Kinnickinnic Avenue

GARFIELD
2933 North 3rd Street
1927-1965
Architects: Dick & Bauer
Seating: 1,800
Organ: 3/11 Barton
Industrial training facility

Detail from the Garfield auditorium ceiling

GARRICK *(See STAR)*
612 North Plankinton Avenue

GARRICK² *(See BIJOU)*
631 North 2nd Street

GAYETY *(See STAR)*
612 North Plankinton Avenue

GAYETY² *(See BIJOU)*
631 North 2nd Street

GAYETY³ *(See NEW STAR)*
755 North 3rd Street

GEM
(Home²)
931 South 5th Street
1909-1938
Architect: Charles Lesser
Seating: 320
Razed

GEM[2] *(See LYRIC*[2]*)*
923 Milwaukee Avenue

GERMAN KINO *(See IRIS)*
2459 West Fond du Lac Avenue

GLOBE
1220 West Walnut Street
1907-1917
Architect: John Menge, Jr.
Seating: 468
Vacant

GRACE
3303 West National Avenue
1911-1957
Architect: Henry Hensel
Seating: 644
Sewing machine facility

GRANADA *(See EMPIRE)*
1125 West Mitchell Street

GRAND
738 North 3rd Street
1904-1909
Architect: John Menge, Jr.
Seating: 800
Remodeled into Princess

GRAND[2]
2917 North Holton Street
1911-1975
Architect: John Roth, Jr.
Seating: 790
Church

GRAND[3]
(Iris[3]*)*
1125 Milwaukee Avenue
1914-1954
Seating: 950
Warehouse/workshop

GRAND[4] (*See WARNER*)
212 West Wisconsin Avenue

GREENDALE
5639 Broad Street
1950-1968
Seating: 600
Store

GREENFIELD
(*Pastime*[2], *Abby*)
2212 West Greenfield Avenue
1913-1957
Architect: Arthur Kienappel
Seating: 530
Meeting hall

HALE'S TOURS (*See SCENES OF THE WORLD*)
184 West Wisconsin Avenue

HAPPY HOUR
1814 Muskego Avenue
1910-1924
Seating: 590
Razed

HOLLYWOOD
(*Coronet*)
3832 North Green Bay Avenue
1924-1959
Architect: John Bruecker
Seating: 748
Razed

HOME (*See TROWBRIDGE*)
2827 West Clybourn Street

HOME[2] (*See GEM*)
931 South 5th Street

IDEAL (*See TRINZ ELECTRIC THEATER*[2])
1465 West Fond du Lac Avenue

IDEAL[2] (*See VAUDETTE*[2])
1036 East Brady Street

IDLE HOUR
(*Alamo*)
1037 South 16th Street
1911-1954
Architect: Name illegible on permit
Seating: 680
Appliance store

IMPERIAL (*See ACADEMY OF MUSIC*)
623 North Milwaukee Street

IMPERIAL[2] (*See ARMORY HALL*)
2674 North Richards Street

IMPERIAL[3] *(See TOY)*
720 North 2nd Street

IMPERIAL 5¢ THEATER *(See EMPORIUM)*
626 West Mitchell Street

IOLA ELECTRIC
1023 North 11th Street
1907-1908
Seating: 175
Razed

IRIS
(Castle, Radio, Show, American[2],
German Kino)
2459 West Fond du Lac Avenue
1911-1966
Architect: Charles Lesser
Seating: 838
Church

IRIS[2] *(See BELL)*
1402 West North Avenue

IRIS[3] *(See GRAND*[3]*)*
1125 Milwaukee Avenue

JACKSON
1322 North Jackson Street
1915-1956
Architects: Van Ryn & De Gellecke
Seating: 834
Razed

JUNEAU
609 West Mitchell Street
1910-1965
Architect: Henry Hengels
Seating: 1,097
Organ: 2/5 Wurlitzer
Razed

KOSCIUSZKO
1337 West Lincoln Avenue
1915-1943
Architect: Arthur Swager
Seating: 735
Razed

LAKE
(Bay)
2893 South Delaware Avenue
1926-1956
Architects: Peacock & Frank
Seating: 970
Commercial/residential

LAYTON/LAYTON PARK *(See BOULEVARD)*
2275 South Layton Boulevard

LEGION (*See WRIGHT*)
734 East Wright Street

LEXINGTON (*See FRANKLIN*)
1706 West Center Street
1911-1961
Architect: Gustave Dick
Seating: 538
Razed

LIBERTY
2623 West Vliet Street
1911-1966
Architect: Henry Hengels
Seating: 493
Razed

LINCOLN
1104 West Lincoln Avenue
1910-1955
Architect: Stanley Kadow
Seating: 490
Vacant

LITTLE (*See GARDEN*)
632 North 3rd Street
(Entrance formerly at
235 West Wisconsin Avenue)

LISBON
(*Royal*[2])
2428 West Lisbon Avenue
1910-1920
Architect: Henry Hengels
Seating: 500
Organ: Barton
Razed

LOCUST (*See PULASKI*[2])
821 East Locust Street

LORRAINE (*See OWL*)
1932 West Fond du Lac Avenue

LIBERTY $2,435.00

LYCEUM *(See ACADEMY OF MUSIC)*

LYCEUM² *(See BELL)*
1402 West North Avenue

LYRIC
311 West Wisconsin Avenue
1908-1913
Architects: Ferry & Clas
Seating: 250
Variety store

LYRIC²
(Gem²)
923 Milwaukee Avenue
1909-1911
Seating: 188
Beauty parlor

LYRIC[3]
3804 West Vliet Street
1917-1952
Architect: John Menge, Jr.
Seating: 575
Carpet store

MAGNET (*See VAUDETTE*)
735 North 3rd Street

MAJESTIC
219 West Wisconsin Avenue
1908-1932
Architects: Kirchhoff & Rose
Seating: 1,902
Bank/office building

MAJESTIC[2]
(*Oakland*[2])
4768 South Packard Avenue
1910-1933
Seating: 500
Razed

MAJESTIC[3]
3620 East Layton Avenue
1927-1980
Architect: Myles Belongia
Seating: 742
Medical complex

MARS (*See ELITE*)
3240 North Green Bay Avenue

MERRILL
211 West Wisconsin Avenue
1915-1930
Architects: Brust & Phillips
Seating: 1,298
Razed

MERRILL PARK
455 North 35th Street
1916-1930
Seating: 450
Razed

MID CITY *(See WHITE HOUSE)*
739 North 3rd Street

MIDGET *(See CENTRAL)*
1662 South 8th Street

MILLER
(Towne)
717 North 3rd Street
1917-1979
Architects: Wolff & Ewens
Seating: 1,700
Razed

H. S. MILLER
2200 North 12th Street
1909-1910
Seating: 250
Razed

MILWAUKEE
(Capitol[2], Ritz[2], National[4], Apollo[2])
2754 North Teutonia Avenue
1921-1975
Architects: Dick & Bauer
Seating: 1,140
Organ: 2/9 Wurli-Bart
Razed

MIRAMAR
(Oakland)
2842 North Oakland Avenue
1913-1954
Architect: George Ehlers
Seating: 800
Community center

MIRTH
2651 South Kinnickinnic Avenue
1913-1952
Architect: William Buscher
Seating: 870
Nightclub

MODJESKA
1124 West Mitchell Street
1910-1923
Architect: Henry Lotter
Seating: 900
Razed for Modjeska²

MODJESKA²
1124 West Mitchell Street
1924-Present
Architects: Rapp & Rapp
Seating: 2,000
Organ: Barton
Operating as theater

MOJUVATE
(*White House²*)
1002 Madison Avenue
1910-1920
Seating: 450
Razed

MOZART
1316 South 16th Street
1910-1952
Architect: Peter Christiansen
Seating: 433
Variety store

MURRAY
(*East*)
2342 North Murray Avenue
1911-1952
Architects: Schutz & Seeler
Seating: 638
Razed

MYSTIC (*See Wauwatosa Theater Delight*)
7208 West State Street

NATIONAL
(*Palace, Palace Pictures, Ace*)
905 South 5th Street
1906-1938
Architect: Charles Lesser
Seating: 266
Sausage factory

NATIONAL²
1610 West National Avenue
1911-1912
Architect: Charles Lesser
Seating: 390
Razed

NATIONAL³
2616 West National Avenue
1928-1971
Architects: Dick & Bauer
Seating: 1,388
Organ: 3/10 Barton
Razed

NATIONAL⁴ (*See MILWAUKEE*)
2754 North Teutonia Avenue

NEW STAR
(*Saxe, Gayety³, Orpheum, Empress²*)
755 North 3rd Street
1906-1955
Architects: Kirchhoff & Rose
Seating: 1,500
Razed

NEWSREEL (*See GARDEN*)
632 North 3rd Street
(Entrance formerly at
235 W. Wisconsin Avenue)

OAKLAND (*See MIRAMAR*)
2842 North Oakland Avenue

OAKLAND[2] *(See MAJESTIC*[2]*)*
4768 South Packard Avenue

OASIS *(See SAVOY)*
2626 West Center Street

OGDEN *(See STUDIO)*
816 East Ogden Avenue

OLYMPIA *(See TRINZ ELECTRIC THEATER*[2]*)*
1465 West Fond du Lac Avenue

OLYMPIC *(See CASINO)*
704 West Walnut Street

ORIENTAL
2230 North Farwell Avenue
1927-Present
Architects: Dick & Bauer
Seating: 2,110
Organ: 3/14 Barton
Operating as theater

*The Oriental
auditorium*

ORPHEUM (*See THEATER DELIGHT*)
203 West Wisconsin Avenue

ORPHEUM[2] (*See PALACE*[3])
535 West Wisconsin Avenue

ORPHEUM[3] (*See NEW STAR*)
755 North 3rd Street

OWL
(*Lorraine*)
1932 West Fond du Lac Avenue
1911-1923
Architect: Charles Lesser
Seating: 480
Butcher shop

PABST
114 East Wells Street
1895-Present
Architect: Otto Strack
Seating: 1,750
Organ: Ferrand & Votey Electro-Pneumatic
Operating as a legitimate theater

PALACE (*See NATIONAL*)
905 South 5th Street

PALACE² (*See COLONIAL*)
1023 Milwaukee Avenue

PALACE³
(*Orpheum²*)
535 West Wisconsin Avenue
1915-1974
Architects: Kirchhoff & Rose
Seating: 2,437
Organ: Wangerin
Razed

PALACE PICTURES (*See NATIONAL*)
905 South 5th Street

PARADISE (*See TOY*)
720 North 2nd Street

PARADISE²
6229 West Greenfield Avenue
1926-Present
Architect: Urban Peacock
Seating: 1,239
Organ: Barton
Operating as theater

PARAMOUNT (*See QUEEN*)
3302 West North Avenue

PARIS
2202 West Center Street
1911-1930
Architect: Herman Schnetzky
Seating: 520
Church

PARK

725 West Mitchell Street
1907-1954
Architect: Henry Lotter
Seating: 405
Furniture store

PARKWAY

(*Rock River*)
3417 West Lisbon Avenue
1931-1986
Architect: Rosman & Wierdsma
Seating: 994
Vacant

PASTIME

(*Warren*)
2614 West North Avenue
1910-1929
Seating: 593
Razed

PASTIME[2] (*See GREENFIELD*)

2212 West Greenfield Avenue

PEARL

1700 South 19th Street
1917-1957
Architect: Herman Buemming
Seating: 660
Warehouse

PEERLESS

917 Monroe Avenue
1907-1908
Razed

PEERLESS[2]

424 East Center Street
1913-1958
Seating: 454
Razed

PENNY ARCADE (*See WONDERLAND SCENIC*)
739 North 3rd Street

PIX (*See AVENUE*)
2311 South Howell Avenue

PLAYER (*See COLONIAL*)
1023 Milwaukee Avenue

PLAZA
3067 South 13th Street
1927-1959
Architect: Arthur Kienappel
Seating: 1,308
Organ: 2 Manual Marr & Colton
Razed

POLA NEGRI (*See CENTRAL*)
1662 South 8th Street

POPULARITY (*See CENTRAL*)
1662 South 8th Street

PRINCESS
738 North 3rd Street
1909-1984
Architect: Henry Lotter
(Remodeled GRAND theater)
Seating: 900
Organ: Barton
Razed

PRINCESS[2]
3531 West Villard Avenue
1912-1925
Seating: 250
Razed

PRINCESS[3] (*See WAUWATOSA THEATER DELIGHT*)
7208 West State Street

PULASKI (*See CENTRAL*)
1662 South 8th Street

PULASKI[2]
(*Locust*)
821 East Locust Street
1911-1919
Architect: Robert Messmer
Seating: 358
Grocery store

QUEEN
(*Paramount, Tivoli*)
3302 West North Avenue
1910-1952
Architect: Charles Lesser
Seating: 500
Warehouse

RADIO (*See IRIS*)
2459 West Fond du Lac Avenue

RAINBOW
2718 West Lisbon Avenue
1911-1965
Architect: Wesley Hess
Seating: 603
Razed

REGAL (*See ROSE*)
704 West Walnut Street

REGENT
4011 West North Avenue
1915-1929
Architect: Arthur Swager
Seating: 878
Bowling alley

REX (*See UNION ELECTRIC*)
2161 South Kinnickinnic Avenue

RIALTO
316 West Wisconsin Avenue
1921-1925
Architects: Kirchhoff & Rose
Seating: 834
Razed

RIALTO²
(*Garden²*)
1005 Milwaukee Avenue
1920-1976
Seating: 750
Carpet store

RITZ
(*Villa*)
3610 West Villard Avenue
1926-1986
Seating: 840
Organ: Kilgen
Vacant

RITZ² (*See MILWAUKEE*)
2754 North Teutonia Avenue

RIVERSIDE
116 West Wisconsin Avenue
1929-Present
Architects: Kirchhoff & Rose
Seating: 2,557
Organ: 3/13 Wurlitzer 235 Special
Operating as special events theater

RIVIERA
1005 West Lincoln Avenue
1921-1954
Architect: Charles Lesser
Seating: 1,200
Organ: 2/5 Wurlitzer
Warehouse

RIVOLI (*See SILVER CITY GEM*)
3506 West National Avenue

ROCK RIVER (*See PARKWAY*)
3417 West Lisbon Avenue

ROOSEVELT (*See BELL*)
1402 West North Avenue

ROSE
(Regal)
704 West Walnut Street
1917-1924 and 1939-1958
Architect: George Zagel
Seating: 500
Razed

ROXY *(See ELITE)*
3240 North Green Bay Avenue

ROYAL
(Aetna)
3000 North 12th Street
1909-1913
Seating: 244
Razed

ROYAL[2] *(See LISBON)*
2428 West Lisbon Avenue

ROYAL[3] *(See WORLD)*
830 South 6th Street

SAVOY
(Oasis)
2626 West Center Street
1914-1975
Architect: Martin Tullgren
Seating: 860
Billiard hall

SAXE *(See NEW STAR)*
755 North 3rd Street

SCENES OF THE WORLD
(Hale's Tours)
184 West Wisconsin Avenue
1905-1906
Seating: 50
Remodeled into THEATORIUM

SCHULTZ BROTHERS ELECTRIC THEATER
2005 West Vliet Street
1906-1907
Seating: 175
Razed

SHERMAN
4632 West Burleigh Street
1935-1977
Architect: Herbert Tullgren
Seating: 995
Church

SHOREWOOD
4329 North Oakland Avenue
1929-1952
Architect: George Zagel
Seating: 1,136
Razed

SHOW (*See IRIS*)
2459 West Fond du Lac Avenue

SHUBERT (*See ACADEMY OF MUSIC*)
623 North Milwaukee Street

SILVER CITY GEM
(*Rivoli*)
3506 West National Avenue
1911-1929
Architect: Charles Lesser
Seating: 462
Office/warehouse

STAR
(*Gayety, Garrick*)
612 North Plankinton Avenue
1899-1909
Architects: Kirchhoff & Rose
Seating: 2,000
Razed

STAR[2] (*See TRINZ ELECTRIC THEATER[2]*)
1465 West Fond du Lac Avenue

STATE
2616 West State Street
1915-1955
Architect: Frank Andree
Seating: 967
Organ: Kimball
Nightclub

STRAND
510 West Wisconsin Avenue
1914-1978
Architects: Wolff & Ewens
Seating: 2,000
Organ: Wangerin-Weickhardt
Razed

STUDIO
(Ogden)
816 East Ogden Avenue
1926-1965
Seating: 586
Razed

SYNDICATE ELECTRIC
2480 West Walnut Street
1907-1908
Seating: 250
Auto body shop/garage

TELENEWS
(Esquire)
310 West Wisconsin Avenue
1947-1981
Architect: Ralph Phillips
Seating: 471
Razed

THEATER DELIGHT
(Orpheum)
203 West Wisconsin Avenue
1907-1913
Seating: 340
Razed

THEATORIUM
184 West Wisconsin Avenue
1906-1923
Seating: 242
Razed

TIMES
5906 West Vliet Street
1935-Present
Architect: Paul Bennett
Seating: 500
Operating as theater

TIVOLI (*See QUEEN*)
3302 West North Avenue

TOSA
6823 West North Avenue
1931-Present
Architect: Paul Bennett
Seating: 560
Operating as theater

TOWER
757 North 27th Street
1926-1975
Architects: Dick & Bauer
Seating: 1,609
Organ: 3/10 Barton
Hospital annex

TOWNE (*See MILLER*)
717 North 3rd Street

TOY
(*Paradise, Imperial*[3])
720 North 2nd Street
1915-1924
Architect: Alexander Guth
Seating: 460
Razed

TRINZ ELECTRIC THEATER
1202 West Mitchell Street
1906-1907
Architect: Nicholas Dornbach
Seating: 247
Fabric/upholstery store

TRINZ ELECTRIC THEATER[2]
(Fond du Lac Electric, Olympia, Ideal, Star[2]*)*
1465 West Fond du Lac Avenue
1906-1914
Architect: Nicholas Dornbach
Seating: 300
Razed

TROWBRIDGE
(Home)
2827 West Clybourn Street
1910-1913
Seating: 250
Razed

UNION ELECTRIC
(Rex, Airdome, Badger)
2161 South Kinnickinnic Avenue
1906-1919
Seating: 275
Apartment/store building

UNIQUE
2355 North 3rd Street
1909-1915
Seating: 188
Razed

UNIQUE[2] *(See WAUWATOSA THEATER DELIGHT)*
7208 West State Street

UNIQUE ELECTRIC
1012 West Mitchell Street
February-April 1907
Seating: 73
Razed

UNIVERSAL *(See WAGNER)*
1636 West Forest Home Avenue

UPTOWN
2323 North 49th Street
1926-1981
Architects: Rapp & Rapp
Seating: 1,818
Organ: 3/10 Barton
Vacant

VARSITY
1326 West Wisconsin Avenue
1938-1976
Architects: Grassold & Johnson
Seating: 1,114
Remodeled into Marquette theater/
lecture hall

VAUDETTE
(Magnet)
735 North 3rd Street
1908-1923
Seating: 492
Razed

VAUDETTE[2]
(Ideal[2], Cozy)
1036 East Brady Street
1908-1914
Seating: 168
Razed

VENETIAN
3629 West Center Street
1927-1954
Architects: Peacock & Frank
Seating: 1,430
Organ: 2/8 Wurlitzer
Liquor store

VENUS
3329 North Green Bay Avenue
1918-1928
Architect: John Bruecker
Seating: 499
Razed

VICTORIA
1037 West Winnebago Street
1911-1918
Seating: 664
Razed

VILLA (*See RITZ*)
3610 West Villard Avenue

VIOLET
2450 West Vliet Street
1915-1956
Architect: Edward Kozick
Seating: 546
Razed

WAGNER
(*Universal*)
1636 West Forest Home Avenue
1913-1917
Architects: Herbst & Hufschmidt
Seating: 371
Vacant

WARNER
(*Centre, Grand*[4])
212 West Wisconsin Avenue
1931-Present
Architects: Rapp & Rapp
Seating: 2,431
Organ: 3/28 Kimball
Operating as theater

WARREN (*See PASTIME*)
2614 West North Avenue

WASHINGTON
3516 West Lisbon Avenue
1911-1923
Architect: Theodore Schutz
Seating: 404
Razed

WAUWATOSA THEATER DELIGHT
(*Princess*[3], *Unique*[2], *Mystic*, *Cozy*[2])
7208 West State Street
1911-1922
Seating: 400
Tavern

WEST SIDE TURN HALL
(*Columbia*)
1023 West Walnut Street
1880-1936
Architects: Rau & Kirsch
Seating: 1,600
Razed

WHITE HOUSE
(*Mid City, Atlantic*)
739 North 3rd Street
1916-1955
Architect: Henry Lotter
Seating: 1,365
Organ: Schuelke
Razed

WHITE HOUSE[2] *(See MOJUVATE)*
1002 Madison Avenue

WHITE HOUSE[3] *(See COLISEUM)*
4763 South Packard Avenue

WISCONSIN
(Cinemas 1 and 2)
530 West Wisconsin Avenue
1924-1986
Architects: Rapp & Rapp
Seating: 3,275
Organ: 3/17 Barton
Razed

WONDERLAND SCENIC
(Penny Arcade)
739 North 3rd Street
1906-1914
Seating: 500
Razed

WORLD
(Royal[3]*)*
830 South 6th Street
1928-1985
Architects: Gurda & Gurda
Seating: 832
Vacant

WRIGHT
(Legion)
734 East Wright Street
1910-1944
Architect: Henry Hengels
Seating: 414
Community hall

ZENITH
2498 North Hopkins Street
1926-1954
Architects: LaCroix & Memmler
Seating: 1,363
Organ: Kilgen
Church

UPTOWN

MUSICAL ~RCE
"WHY LEAVE HOME"
KING OF KONGO

SUE CAROL "WHY LEAVE HOME"
FOX MOVIETONE NEWS-IT SPEAKS

UPTOWN

25
Anniversary

ILLUSTRATION CREDITS:

All illustrations are from the authors' collection except for the following, which are reproduced courtesy of:

Marjorie Albert, p. 43
Bay View Historical Society, p. 10
William Boehnlein, p. 29
Arnold Brumm, p. 103 (top)
The Emil B. LaCroix Architectural Archives, pp. 64-65
Ben Marcus, pp. 96, 111
Sid Margoles, p. 115
Frances Maertz, p. 94
Milwaukee County Historical Society, pp. 4, 6, 7, 9, 11, 18-19, 22, 24, 33, 46, 58, 60, 80, 82-83, 97, 110 (top), 145
Milwaukee Public Library, pp. 16, 44, 55, 74, 108, 153, 168
Milwaukee Sentinel, pp. 118-119
Elmer Nimmer, p. 104
Poblocki & Sons, p. 140
Theater Historical Society of America, pp. 61, 62, 68, 70-71, 75, 120, 129, 148
Edward Trinz, p. 27
UWM Special Collections, Golda Meir Library, p. 26
Jessie Walker, pp. 20, 37, 38, 114

PHOTOGRAPHIC CREDITS:

Joseph Brown, p. 20
Alfred Breitwish, p. 110 (top)
Chicago Architectural Photographing Co., pp. 61, 62, 68, 70-71, 75, 120, 129, 148
Hedrich-Blessing, p. 114
Carl Hoyt, pp. 118-119
Jaksch Studios, p. 34
Roman Kwasniewski, p. 26
Albert Kuhli, pp. 23, 30, 32, 42, 45, 46, 48, 49, 54, 56, 58, 64-65, 66, 79, 81, 88, 92, 96, 99, 111, 131, 149, 151, 156, 168
Milwaukee Commercial Photographers, p. 97
James Murdoch, pp. 59, 86, 101, 103, 107, 110 (bottom), 137, 140, 142, 145, 158
Fred Stanger, pp. 105, 165
John Taylor, pp. 24, 98
Albert Toepfer, pp. 82-83
Larry Widen, pp. 73, 76, 78, 84, 85, 87, 112, 113, 116, 117, 135

SOURCES

Books:

Austin, Russell. *The Milwaukee Story*. Milwaukee: The Milwaukee Journal Co., 1946.

Gardiner, Helen. *Art Through the Ages*. 7th ed. New York: Harcourt Brace Jovanovich, Inc., 1980.

Grau, Robert. *The Business Man in the Amusement World*. New York: Broadway Publishing Co., 1910.

Hall, Ben M. *The Best Remaining Seats*. New York: Clarkson N. Potter, Inc., 1961.

Hartt, Frederick. *History of Italian Renaissance Art*. New York: Prentice-Hall/Abrams, 1979.

Lindsay, Vachel. *The Art of the Moving Picture*. New York: Liveright Publishing, 1970.

Milwaukee Towne Corporation v. Loews, Inc., et al.; Vol. VI. United States Court of Appeals for the Seventh Circuit, 1945.

Naylor, David. *American Picture Palaces*. New York: Van Nostrand Reinhold Co., 1981.

Ramsaye, Terry. *A Million and One Nights*. New York: Simon and Schuster, 1923.

Sennett, Mack, and Cameron Shipp. *King of Comedy*. Garden City, New York: Doubleday, 1954.

Sexton, R. W., ed. *American Theaters of Today*. New York: Architectural Book Publishing Co., Inc., 1930.

Still, Bayrd. *Milwaukee: The History of a City*. Madison: State Historical Society of Wisconsin, 1948.

Transportation Survey. Milwaukee Metropolitan District. Mclellan & Junkersfield, Inc., Engineers, 1927.

Treasures of Tutankhamen. New York: Metropolitan Museum of Art, 1976.

Correspondence:

To authors from Lillian Gish, actress; Hildegarde, performer; Claire-Lisette Hubbard, last Princess owner; Robert Rothschild, retired film distributor; Edward Trinz, son of Henry Trinz.

From RKO Distribution Corporation to Michael Brumm, manager, Ritz theater.